STUDIES IN FRENCH LIT

General Edit

W. G. Moore

BAUDELAIRE:
LES FLEURS DU MAL

by

ALISON FAIRLIE

Fellow of Girton College and Professor of French,
University of Cambridge

EDWARD ARNOLD

© ALISON FAIRLIE 1960

First published 1960 by
Edward Arnold (Publishers) Ltd,
41 Bedford Square, London WC1B 3DP
Reprinted 1965, 1969, 1972, 1975, 1978

ISBN: 0 7131 5512 4

Printed and bound in Great Britain at
The Camelot Press Ltd, Southampton

Contents

PART I

PART II

Introduction

If one single volume had to be chosen through which to approach French poetry, the *Fleurs du Mal* might be the most rewarding. No delicate web of classical convention or of symbolist obscurity separates its immediate meaning from the modern or the foreign reader. Yet it is also poetry where on each re-reading new and rich undertones come to stimulate the mind, the feelings and the senses. It has been called the pivot on which European poetry of the nineteenth century turns towards the future, but it also enriches themes familiar through centuries of tradition by its own intensely individual variations. And, although each poem stands to be enjoyed in its own right, this is not just a collection of separate pieces, but a book deliberately arranged to give from birth to death the outline of a human destiny.

At intervals in French literature there has appeared a strikingly original poet, original not because he rejected what came before him, but because he formed something distinctively his own from the rich and complex resources of past tradition and contemporary experiment. In their century, Racine and La Fontaine were poets of this kind. Baudelaire's greatness does not lie, as is sometimes suggested, in novelty of themes or theories. Many of his subjects are those common to a romantic age: *ennui*, revolt, the function and sufferings of the poet. The more apparently startling—the macabre, drugs, lesbianism, sadism, satanism—were familiar currency among novelists and minor poets in his day. In artistic theories he takes up and develops with acute and provocative intelligence ideas that were in the air in his time.

Baudelaire detested the *poncif*—the mechanical, lofty and lifeless imitation of ancient or fashionable models—but he found in past and present countless traditions which could be brought alive in a new way. His age had rediscovered the sixteenth-century poets of the Pléiade and the 'grotesque' or 'libertin' poets of the early seventeenth century; he transfers to a modern world something of their courtly sensuousness, virulent cruelty or macabre terror. From the classical world, memories of the mourning Andromache, of the exiled Ovid or of the subtle love poetry of a hyper-civilised age are made part of the aspiration and anguish of contemporary Paris with its mud and fog and rubble. The undertones of religious ritual, its litanies of supplication, worship and terror, are called on in the strange contexts of poems on love, disgust, and revolt. Romanticism too offered possibilities which had not been fully used: possibilities of intimacy, familiarity, and suggestion. And painting and music (particularly painting) were often a vital stimulus to his ideas and practice as a poet.

It is not as the first poet ever to discover the life of the modern city, decay, perversity or the theory of the *Correspondances* that Baudelaire matters. He creates a new kind of poetry because of his particularly penetrating insight into central human struggles and his mastery of the art of suggestion.

The first part of this brief study suggests a general approach to the *Fleurs du Mal*; the second follows the poems in the order in which Baudelaire wished them to be read, an order he considered essential to the full understanding of his meaning and his art. In the first edition, in 1857, he had only partly worked out this plan, and many of the poems had not yet been written. The third edition was published after his death, in 1868, and in it a good many later poems were inserted without much thought for the place Baudelaire would have given them. The second edition (1861) was carefully arranged by Baudelaire himself and is the nearest to what he intended; it was of course incomplete in not containing the six poems condemned by the prosecution of 1857, and others written after the 1861 edition or for various reasons not included in it. Most modern editors follow the order established by Baudelaire in 1861, and place these other poems in groups at the end. It is this order which will be followed here, with the poems from *Les Epaves* discussed at the point where Baudelaire had intended them to appear.

Page references are those of the Pléiade revised edition, 1961.

PART I

1. Poetry and the Nature of Man

In his ideas on poetry, Baudelaire does not start from philosophical theories or mystical beliefs, but from observing human experience. There are moments in everyone's life, he says, when we feel our vitality intensified so that any object we look at, however trivial, seems to hold delight and meaning, strikes our senses strongly and suggests a train of ideas. The child has this sense of the sharpness and wonder of experience; prolonged nervous tension may provoke the same heightening of sensitivity, as in the man who is returning to life after illness; it may be produced by the artificial stimulus of alcohol or drugs. But in none of these states can one prolong or express the ecstasy felt. It is poetry which can deliberately create and sustain this almost magic sense of intensity and meaning in ordinary things, an 'enthousiasme des sens et de l'esprit' (pp. 347–50, 974, 1158–9, 1257).

But such moments are rare, and in contrast there stretch 'les lourdes ténèbres de l'existence journalière'. Then time seems to crawl endlessly and monotonously by in a world without meaning, or ticks past at relentless speed, each moment a reproach for stagnation and uselessness. Trying to throw off the weight of lethargy, man may turn to whatever offers intense stimulus, and find even the stab of horror or disgust preferable to drab indifference. This too may be the material for poetry, for

> c'est un des privilèges prodigieux de l'Art que l'horrible, artistement exprimé, devienne beauté et que la *douleur* rhythmée et cadencée remplisse l'esprit d'une *joie* calme (695).

The core of Baudelaire's poetry is the struggle between appetite and apathy. His own nature is rooted in this: he describes himself as 'un paresseux nerveux' (1296)—a man of restless and clamant sensibility constantly falling back into indolence and procrastination. For him, the most crucial problem is how to make poetry of the moments of delight or terror he experiences; inertia in the inner world and time in the outer world threaten him with failure to create:

> Quand saurai-je donc faire
> Du spectacle vivant de ma triste misère
> Le travail de mes mains et l'amour de mes yeux? (15).

In his catalogue of vices (*Au Lecteur*) not lechery but lethargy has chief place,[1] and constantly will-power and work are the means of salvation. To the theme of the sapping of will-power, man's most precious possession, he gives his most piercing and terrifying images: the will is stifled or battered, swept off by avalanche or buried in slime, eaten away and corroded, rocked and lulled into indifference, or vaporised into a wisp of smoke.

When Baudelaire insisted that the poet should express the spirit of his age, and praised the romantics for giving to literature new possibilities that they had not fully used, he saw as the centre a sense of 'la mélancolie' and 'le malheur'. A line from the *Fleurs du Mal* might well sum up the romantic attitude to the world:

Un monde où l'action n'est pas la sœur du rêve (115).

A consciousness of the discrepancy between desire and reality exists of course in any age, but it may provoke very different reactions. A religious age will accept it as part of a plan in which perfection exists only in another life; a classical age will give it balanced analysis as a necessary and permanent consequence of the nature of things (and may often draw from it serene or biting comedy as in Molière, or in La Fontaine with his amused matter-of-course 'Mais qui peut tout avoir?'); an age of social reform will concentrate on decreasing the gap between ideal and real. In the nineteenth century a series of revolutions has failed to reach the millennium, and for many men religious faith has given way to doubt or to the Twilight of the Gods. The theme of longing for the infinite, 'la recherche de l'absolu', takes on a new prominence and a new anguish. But in several ways it may produce doubtful art. The temptation to ringing but empty laments is strong; vague visions of an ideal paradise fail to bring alive anything but a diffuse and magniloquent longing. At the opposite extreme there may be mere versified philosophy. And, worst of temptations, there is the spurious glorification of the hero dissatisfied with the nature of things. Either he is the innocent victim of evil circumstances, or his faults, if faults he has, are made lofty and abstract, transformed by grandiose oratory into a kind of virtue; the effort is constantly to disarm criticism and attract the reader's

---

[1] Another great writer analysing human nature had seen in *la Paresse* the most insinuating and the most deadly of man's vices. It is worth reading La Rochefoucauld's Maxims 266 and 630 (Pléiade edition) side by side with *Au Lecteur*.

sentimental complicity. Baudelaire's treatment of man's failure to achieve his infinite aspirations produces something that is in several ways very different.

His is no vague idealised longing. He sees clearly how man's appetites seek to go beyond the necessary limits of human existence, the limits of time, space and individuality; how he tries to 'vivre plusieurs vies d'homme en l'espace d'une heure', to 'allonger les heures par l'infini des sensations', to have 'dans le présent le passé restauré', to penetrate the existence of other beings and yet remain himself. Man seeks to reach the absolute, to become godlike, and yet to retain his individual consciousness. This is an old philosophical dilemma, and Baudelaire is well aware of its contradiction. The condition of individual existence is imperfection; to have reached infinity would be to lose one's separate personality:

Les poètes, les artistes et toute la race humaine seraient bien malheureux, si l'idéal, cette absurdité, cette impossibilité, était trouvé. Qu'est-ce que chacun ferait désormais de son pauvre moi? (912).

Poetry then does not achieve any infinite, does not give man a metaphysical revelation nor describe a supernatural paradise. It expresses the dreams and longings of imperfect man as he is.

How, in any case, can finite man convey a sense of the infinite? Beyond vague abstractions, what can be said of it? In a letter Baudelaire remarks that the best way of giving an impression of infinite distance is to show the endless depths of sky framed in a small opening, set between chimneys or seen through the limiting outline of a window or a grating. So the sense of ecstasy is conveyed by setting it side by side with the reality from which it is formed and into which it falls back; the sense of striving towards perfection is best given not through philosophical or emotional abstractions but through the suggestive use of the trivial, frail and limited objects of the world as we know it.

Baudelaire constantly chooses from human experience themes, feelings and images which call up far-stretching possibilities and irreducible refusals. When woman is cold and distant she takes on a bitter loveliness as she evokes the longing for the unattainable:

Et t'aime d'autant plus, belle, que tu me fuis,
Et que tu me parais, ornement de mes nuits,
Plus ironiquement accumuler les lieues
Qui séparent mes bras des immensités bleues; (26)

when she shows herself insatiable in her physical demands she suggests man's desperate effort towards the impossible. Certain tiny, apparently limited and exactly outlined objects fascinate Baudelaire because he can make of them the finite frame for something with endless prolongations. Jewels, tinkling together on a chain, take on infinite reverberations of sound and light:

> ses bijoux sonores . . .
> Ce monde rayonnant de métal et de pierre
> Me ravit en extase, et j'aime à la fureur
> Les choses où le son se mêle à la lumière (142).

and the eye, that tiny part of the human body, both looks out into limitless distance and seems to stretch inwardly into impenetrable depths, reflecting subtle changes of light and shade, until it becomes the emblem of what is indefinable and unfathomable.

The longing and the dream in Baudelaire are not erected into any super-reality or falsely glorified. The desire for an unrealisable perfection is man's highest dignity but also his most dangerous temptation: 'Tout homme qui n'accepte pas les conditions de la vie vend son âme.' Where often the romantics, in setting man against circumstance, had given un-alloyed sympathy to the hero, Baudelaire turns the focus of criticism from the outer force to the inner flaw. Where they either stigmatise evil outside themselves, or present noble failings seen on a grandiose scale, Baude-laire plunges himself and the 'hypocrite lecteur, mon semblable, mon frère' into the complexity, the pettiness and the insinuating tenacity of the less easily avowable sins. The opening lines of *Au Lecteur*:

> La sottise, l'erreur, le péché, la lésine,
> Occupent nos esprits et travaillent nos corps . . .

use the dignified terms 'erreur' and 'péché' but flank them by words less easily acceptable—'la sottise' and 'la lésine': pig-headed stupidity and stingy niggardliness, with the very sound of the words conveying a hissing scorn; and they lead on to expose the self-congratulation inherent even in self-loathing:

> Et nous alimentons nos aimables remords
> Comme les mendiants nourrissent leur vermine.

Through his images Baudelaire ruthlessly lays bare all that is suspect as well as all that is great in man's dissatisfactions and regrets.

This brings us to the relation between poetry and morality. The theory of *l'art pour l'art* had been suggested by Hugo (soon to turn away from it) in the first Preface to the *Orientales* (1829) and given brilliant and deliberately paradoxical form in Gautier's preface to *Mademoiselle de*

Maupin (1834); in the middle of the century Leconte de Lisle, Flaubert and Baudelaire argue out their individual views. The doctrine is often wrongly seen as denying any contact between art and morality; even Gautier, when not rejoicing in the fireworks of anti-propagandist propaganda or simulating superior indolence, produced the flat but clear line: 'Menez le peuple au bien par le chemin du Beau', and Leconte de Lisle held that by returning to impartial description of ancient beauty the poet would contribute to the finer future of humanity. What these loosely associated authors have in common amounts perhaps to three beliefs, which must be seen against the background of an age that prosecuted the *Fleurs du Mal* and *Madame Bovary*. The artist should not have direct teaching as his aim; he should realise that good intentions are valueless without the expression that brings them alive; his work must not be judged simply by superficial or conventional moral standards.

To Baudelaire explicit moralising is unnecessary and intrusive: a great work of art will necessarily provoke reflections, and it is the merest politeness to assume that the reader can do his own judging. In a letter to Swinburne he writes:

> Je ne suis pas si *moraliste* que vous feignez obligeamment de le croire. Je crois simplement que tout poème, tout objet d'art *bien fait* suggère naturellement et forcément une morale. C'est l'affaire du lecteur. J'ai même une haine très décidée contre toute intention morale exclusive dans un poème.

Not only does explicit moralising intrude on the experience; it may also, if ill-conceived, falsify it. To present the world as if virtue always triumphed, Baudelaire says in his attack on the moralising dramatists of the *théâtre utile*, is to produce not only distorted art but distorted morality; it is like persuading a child to be good only because he will be given a sweet as a reward, and exposing him to the disillusion of the world as it is. To present evil as automatically and simply repulsive is to falsify the nature of things:

> L'art est-il utile? Oui. Pourquoi? Parce qu'il est l'art. Y a-t-il un art pernicieux? Oui. C'est celui qui dérange les conditions de la vie. Le vice est séduisant, il faut le peindre séduisant; mais il traîne avec lui des maladies et des douleurs morales singulières; il faut les décrire (620).

The artist's intention is not to force on the reader his own views, but to express piercingly and honestly the complexity of an experience. Baudelaire sums up when he writes: 'Aucun poème ne sera si grand, si noble, que celui qui aura été écrit uniquement pour le plaisir d'écrire un poème' (685).

It is easier today than in the mid-nineteenth century to take for granted the poet's right to choose any subject and leave conclusions to the reader. But Baudelaire is too often forced into comforting, over-simple moral categories. He has been seen as a modern mystic, as funda-mentally a religious believer in whom revolt and blasphemy are a sign of ingrained faith, as the social critic of a collapsing civilisation, as the unselfish lover of the poor and the outcast. His insight into human nature and his own nature is a good deal more probing and uncomfortable than some of these simplifications would suggest.

Baudelaire is neither the mystic nor the decadent, the poet of idealism nor the poet of despair. At his centre is the struggle between conflicting urges and opposing possibilities in any experience:

Tout enfant, j'ai senti dans mon cœur deux sentiments contradictoires, l'horreur de la vie et l'extase de la vie (1296);

and: 'Il y a dans tout homme, à toute heure, deux postulations simul-tanées.' But this is no simple antithesis poised in a clear contrast of good and evil. Within any quality Baudelaire will find seeds of its opposite. *Ennui* is both 'la source de toutes vos maladies' and 'la source de tous vos misérables progrès'. Opposing it are the strivings of intellect and imagina-tion, sources of delight and worth, but also of torment and disillusion. The desire for ecstasy is the urge both to intensify and to lose the con-sciousness of self. Remorse and self-immolation may become complacent and loathly self-indulgence; their opposite, pride, has in it the seeds both of a desperate revolt against the nature of things and of the indomitable will to create. The instinct that draws man to his fellows is escapist and self-congratulatory as well as a sign of human solidarity. The very lucidity which analyses man's nature intensifies the contradictions and becomes a cause of torment as well as of pride.

Emotions and sensations reflect the same conflicts. Love includes hatred; cruelty and disgust may make part of tenderness. In *Une Charogne* the same detailed physical sensations which evoke the seething, buzzing, stinking corruption of the carrion are gradually made to suggest what is lovely and lasting. Constantly an idea or an image contains its opposite or gradually moves into that opposite, and this gives Baudelaire's poetry its particular tone of both tension and fluidity.

In a famous passage in *Fusées* (1255), Baudelaire gives his idea of beauty as 'quelque chose d'ardent et de triste . . . laissant carrière à la conjecture'.

He explains this further in an article on Hugo: the writer who wishes to expound the known laws that govern the universe, whether moral or physical, has prose as his instrument; if this is his purpose, verse is a superfluous and dangerous ornamentation, detracting from precision and clarity. But the poet is concerned with 'toutes les rêveries suggérées par le spectacle infini de la vie' and it is his privilege to

traduire, dans un langage magnifique autre que la prose et la musique, les conjectures éternelles de la curieuse humanité[1] (711).

The poetry of the Fleurs du Mal is not simple moralising. Nor is it a decadent world of reversed values. It is a penetrating, lucid and suggestive expression of the complex struggle in man of creative and destructive forces.

If poetry is not for Baudelaire the conveying of a didactic message, neither is it the spontaneous outpouring of passionate feeling. In his notes for a Preface to the Fleurs du Mal he even insists that a poet may write as great a poem on something he has never himself felt as on something he has. What matters is not whether he himself has had the experience, but whether he has the imagination and the power of expression which can create it in the poem. Too strong a feeling may even be dangerous:

La sensibilité de cœur n'est pas absolument favorable au travail poétique. Une extrême sensibilité de cœur peut même nuire en ce cas. La sensibilité de l'imagination est d'une autre nature; elle sait choisir, juger, comparer (688).

Musset had exclaimed 'Ah! frappe-toi le cœur, c'est là qu'est le génie!' Gautier, reacting against open emotionalism and rhetorical outpouring, had in Emaux et Camées not, as is often wrongly thought, excluded all emotion, but reduced it to the muted and undisturbing tone of the ingenious and the graceful. Banville and Leconte de Lisle, in the general movement of mistrust for unleashed feeling, anecdotal indiscretion and flowing style, turn to their own solutions: decorative virtuosity or epic and philosophical disguise. Baudelaire's solution might be summed up by his own remark that there are two fundamental literary qualities: 'surnaturalisme et ironie' (1256).

The capacity to look at themselves ironically is not one of the gifts to be found in the personal poetry of Baudelaire's immediate predecessors;

[1] Valéry's distinction between poetry and prose (Variété III: 'Au Sujet du Cimetière Marin'), so influential in later criticism, is very close to the main points raised by Baudelaire in this passage.

the great French romantics regard their mission and their sufferings as a priesthood. Some attempt at byronic irony does occur in the early poems of Musset and Gautier, but this is the technique of moments of frivolous pirouette; irony stands separate from feeling and at intervals deflates or destroys it, instead of fusing with it and intensifying the seriousness. In Gautier's *Ténèbres* or some poems of Sainte-Beuve a more serious fusion of tones is clumsily attempted, but it is Baudelaire who fully rediscovers how to make the reader share a feeling the more strongly because of the virulent, sardonic and lucid self-criticism which ironically underscores it.

By 'surnaturalisme' Baudelaire does not here mean anything to do with the supernatural as the word is commonly used. He means the use of objects in the material, the 'natural' world as symbols which evoke something other than their physical appearance: in fact, non-naturalistic or suggestive art. Baudelaire most often creates feelings gradually and subtly through sensation and image, rather than by factual anecdote, abstract analysis or intellectual comment. He does, of course, use all of these as well, and brilliantly, but never at length, and the main substance of his poetry is suggestive. *La Chevelure* does not say in abstract emotional terms: 'You are the source of all my aspirations and dreams; you are the centre of peace and consolation'; it starts from the beauty of his mistress's thickly-waving hair, its blue-black sheen and heavy scent, and through the analogy of a ship borne off on the waves of the sea to distant lands evokes ambitions and longings, indolent ecstasy and the return, after delight and weariness, to rest. The *Spleen* poem 'Pluviôse, irrité . . .' does not state or analyse melancholy; at first sight it is simply describing the things round a man in his comfortless room—a mangy cat, a tolling bell, the log smoking on the fire, a ticking clock and a pack of cards, but through these objects it creates nervous exasperation, mental tension, fear, loss, weariness, obsession, regret, menace, disgust, without any need for these abstract terms.

2. Poetry and the Outer World

Poetry to Baudelaire is not impartial description, but a choice of elements from the real world to bring alive an original vision. 'Il ne s'agit pas de copier, mais d'interpréter.' He reacts against the contemporary love of the picturesque, the plastic and the purely decorative, but also gladly quotes writers or artists whose views run parallel with his own:

Edgar Allan Poe, Mrs. Crowe on the creative imagination, and above all Delacroix as seeing in the real world a dictionary from which the artist will choose and arrange the elements he needs: 'une espèce de pâture que l'imagination doit digérer et transformer' (1040-5).

Creative imagination transforms or heightens reality, but it does not reject the real world to float into airy dreams and abstractions; it must not become 'cette chose vague, ce rêve ennuyeux et impalpable'. The poet creates 'une magie suggestive, contenant à la fois le monde extérieur à l'artiste et l'artiste lui-même' (1099). When Baudelaire takes as his subject a beautiful woman, a Paris street scene, the gamblers round the gaming-table or the decrepit old women, he does not describe them in every detail or purely for their own sake, but makes them the means to evoke a mood and the instrument of self-analysis. But the mood is created by his choice of richly evocative details from the physical world, and gives new sharpness and strangeness to the things seen as well as to the feelings they suggest.

In his individual choice of things from the outer world, at one extreme he turns to the love of all kinds of artifice. He refuses to worship Nature and remarks sardonically 'Je suis incapable de m'attendrir sur les végétaux.' This love of artifice stands for conflicting urges. On the one hand it suggests what is highest in man and is the emblem of will-power, for

Tout ce qui est beau et noble est le résultat de la raison et du calcul. Le crime . . . est naturel. La vertu, au contraire, est *artificielle* . . . Le mal se fait sans effort, *naturellement*, par fatalité; le bien est toujours le produit d'un art (1183).

But Baudelaire is perfectly conscious of another attraction in the artificial; hyper-civilised man finds pleasure in the touch of deliberate over-sophistication; pleasure of a kind which may be 'agréable à l'esprit comme les discordances aux oreilles blasées'.

The world of artifice, with its two sides, is evoked by his praise of the coldly-disciplined distinction of the *dandy*, by his love of jewels and cosmetics in women, or by his creating imagined cities of metal and mineral from which all trace of the vegetable world is excluded.

Yet the hyper-civilised often turn with longing to the contrast of a primeval world, and sometimes, wearied by struggle and self-analysis, he will invoke instinctive animal simplicity:

> Mon cœur, que tout irrite,
> Excepté la candeur de l'antique animal . . .
> Je hais la passion et l'esprit me fait mal! . . . (62)

or again suggest the enchantment of a mingling of innocence and sophistication: 'la candeur unie à la lubricité', or 'ta beauté Où l'enfance s'allie à la maturité' (142, 49).

But the love of artifice is counterbalanced by another kind of choice from the outer world. The poet should select what is most 'modern', least familiar to previous tradition, and so most apparently prosaic or ugly:

> Il est beaucoup plus commode de déclarer que tout est absolument laid dans l'habit d'une époque, que de s'appliquer à en extraire la beauté mystérieuse qui y peut être contenue (1163).

The real artist must

> arracher à la vie actuelle son côté épique, et nous faire voir et comprendre . . . combien nous sommes grands et poétiques dans nos cravates et nos bottes vernies (866).

Baudelaire is the first fully to bring alive the poetry of modern everyday life, though here again he is not the first to think of trying. Hugo's claim in the *Préface de Cromwell* that the grotesque as well as the sublime has its place in art still poses the sublime and the grotesque at lofty extremes and in eloquent terms. But the movement to call a spade a spade and to give it a place in poetry had been developing gradually if interruptedly from the second half of the eighteenth century. Sainte-Beuve is the centre of the attempt to give a new sting and a new savour through everyday subjects and a language close to prose yet not prosaic, and at different times Vigny, Gautier and Hugo all try their hand with this material.

But the pseudo-classical tradition of nobility died hard. Those who introduce everyday subjects into their poetry often fail to give 'la beauté mystérieuse qui y peut être contenue', perhaps for three main reasons. On the one hand, half afraid at their audacity in choosing something so prosaic, they feel impelled to ennoble it and deck it out in ornate images which are hideously out of keeping with the subject: Vigny's railway engine in *La Maison du Berger* becomes a dragon, or a roaring bull, and is topped by a blue-eyed angel with drawn sword to ward off dangerous pebbles. (Fundamentally this is the same spirit which attempts to prettify a teapot by giving it the shape of a country cottage.) At the opposite extreme there is the thudding banality of mere versified statement, written under the illusion that to have mentioned an object in verse is to have created poetry: the tone of the flat, matter-of-fact descriptive detail frequent in Sainte-Beuve or Vigny. (Vigny is of course at his best in poetry of another kind; it is interesting that in *La Sauvage* and *La Flûte* he should so deliberately have experimented with this kind of tone.)

It is worth comparing the beginning of *La Flûte*:

> Un jour je vis s'asseoir au pied de ce grand arbre
> Un Pauvre qui posa sur ce vieux banc de marbre
> Son sac et son chapeau, s'empressa d'achever
> Un morceau de pain noir, puis se mit à rêver . . .

with even four lines from Baudelaire's *Les Petites Vieilles:*

> Ils rampent, flagellés par les bises iniques,
> Frémissant au fracas roulant des omnibus,
> Et serrant sur leur flanc, ainsi que des reliques,
> Un petit sac brodé de fleurs ou de rébus. (85)

The first is a series of factual statements; nothing in them brings alive physically the tree, the bench, the 'sac et chapeau' or the gesture of the man; nor, except for the rather obvious 'pain noir', is any of these objects related to the feeling the poet wants to give. In Baudelaire's lines, every touch brings alive both a physical and a mental sense of the grotesque and the pitiful. The forgotten old women have become sexless beings; by calling them earlier 'des monstres disloqués' the poet can for several stanzas refer to them with a kind of neuter 'ils', detaching them from anything feminine. They creep along the streets with the almost animal 'rampent'; the icy winds and thundering buses are given physical force in 'flagellés' and 'fracas roulant', and suggest that the old women are both battered by the elements of nature and terrorised by the civilisation of the city. Instead of the matter-of-fact 'il posa son sac et son chapeau' there is a picture where both physical gesture and mental meaning spring alive in the clumsy clutch on the little embroidered bag, a symbol of the past so precious as to be ridiculously treasured like a religious relic. Here the intensity of the physical suggestions is made an integral part of the feelings roused.

This leads to the third kind of difficulty in the use of objects from the outer world: their function as images or symbols. The image seizes a relationship between two things. It is at its most successful when it shows something vital about both terms in the comparison, and when every detail in the description of either seems essentially relevant to their central likeness. The bottle thrown on the sea with its message in Vigny's *La Bouteille à la Mer* is the emblem for the lasting form of poetry which hands on great ideas to the future; the details of its seal, the kind of wine it once contained, and so on are merely decorative elaboration.

The finest images give a feeling not just of an ingenious intellectual parallel, but of a compelling and suggestive interaction of two things. This is perhaps why the technique of first describing an object in detail or telling a story and then explaining the meaning rarely produces the best poetry. This frequent nineteenth-century device leaves us too conscious of the division between outer and inner worlds, and of the intrusion of an outside observer to explain and discuss. It is still to be found in *l'Albatros* and one or two of Baudelaire's more conventional poems, whereas works like *La Chevelure* or *Le Cygne* move subtly and almost imperceptibly between outer and inner worlds, constantly enriching each by analogies with the other.

The sonnet *Correspondances* has been more argued over than any poem in the *Fleurs du Mal*, and has often been erected into a mystical as well as an aesthetic manifesto. To take first the bare skeleton of its meaning, it suggests two kinds of network of relationships, of 'correspondances'. The objects of the concrete world suggest some abstract meaning (some critics have called these the 'vertical' correspondences); and the different sensations are inter-related, so that a particular scent may correspond to a particular colour or sound (these are sometimes called the 'horizontal' correspondences, and are familiar under the term synaesthesia).

Far from claiming that he had invented these ideas or that he saw anything revolutionary in applying them to poetry, Baudelaire constantly speaks of them as something natural to the poetic imagination. He praises Gautier and Hugo among others for their capacity to seize analogies between the different senses or between the concrete and the abstract. And not only to the poet, but to any man in a state of awareness, sensations will suggest feelings or ideas:

> Qui n'a connu ces admirables heures . . . où les couleurs parlent, où les parfums racontent des mondes d'idées? (974)

Like others in his time (Nerval, Balzac and Hugo among them) Baudelaire is often intrigued by mystical theories which make of the objects of the physical world divinely appointed symbols of a spiritual reality which it is the artist's mission to interpret. But the value of *Correspondances* or the use of images in the *Fleurs du Mal* does not depend on any such theory. Baudelaire's poetry is made not of fixed mathematical relationships between a given object and a metaphysical absolute, but of shifting and variable analogies, chosen to fit individual personality and changing mood; they are not those of a prophet giving a revelation but of an artist showing a personal way of looking at the world. They are the product not of revelation but of imagination.

> L'un t'éclaire avec son ardeur,
> L'autre en toi met son deuil, Nature!
> Ce qui dit à l'un: Sépulture!
> Dit à l'autre: Vie et splendeur! (72)

According to mood, clouds, for example, can be the symbol of the richest delight:

> Les plus grands paysages
> Jamais ne contenaient l'attrait mystérieux
> De ceux que le hasard fait avec les nuages (124)

or of the funeral procession of despair:

> Vos vastes nuages en deuil
> Sont les corbillards de mes rêves . . . (73)

The forests, the sea, the cool starlit shadows of night, each of which had called up joy and aspiration, become in *Obsession* the emblems of torment.

The poem *Correspondances* does not convey any specific mystical message. In its first part it suggests something basic in human experience: the sense of both haunting mystery and significant pattern behind the forms of the natural world. And in the second part it is important to see how Baudelaire has allowed for the individual and the variable in synaesthesia. When pushed to extremes (as in Rimbaud's *Voyelles*) impressions of this kind become purely subjective; interesting phenomena but differing in detail from individual to individual. Baudelaire is both specific enough to stimulate our imagination and general enough to let it create its own analogies; he does not say 'this particular scent is green', but in the first set of comparisons leaves the scents undefined while creating through other sensations an arabesque of purity and peace:

> Il est des parfums frais comme des chairs d'enfants,
> Doux comme les hautbois, verts comme les prairies . . .

and in the second, defines the scents ('musc, benjoin, encens') but suggests their analogies only in the most general terms ('corrompus, riches et triomphants').

Correspondances will gain from being read as a poem rather than a theory. It expresses those moments of delight when both mind and senses stand alert and the mystery behind the world seems just about to be explained. It is a poem of suggestive tensions: between the thronging forms that crowd in on man and his infinite aspirations that stretch and echo into vast distances; between the evocation of purity and peace and the sense of the rich, the heavy and the sultry. It matters, not as a mystical belief, nor even as a new theory of art, but because it shows how Baudelaire will carry to a particular pitch the controlled and subtle use of the sense impressions to suggest each other and to suggest ideas, feelings or moods.

3. The Art of Suggestion

'Manier savamment une langue', said Baudelaire, 'c'est pratiquer une espèce de sorcellerie évocatoire' (690). It is only by the most acute and exact sense of the exciting possibilities of words, their associations, their sounds, and the ways of combining them, that the poet can create ideas, feelings or sensations. 'Il n'y a pas de hasard dans l'art' (890). 'L'imagination est la plus *scientifique* des facultés.' Far from thinking of poetry as a matter of vague divine inspiration separated from man's other activities, he compares it not only to music and to mathematics for the fascination of its controlled patterns, but also to cooking and cosmetics for its capacity to produce the most subtle effects from the most exact gradation of ingredients:

La poésie se rattache aux arts de la peinture, de la cuisine et du cosmétique par la possibilité d'exprimer toute sensation de suavité ou d'amertume, de béatitude ou d'horreur, par l'accouplement de tel substantif avec tel adjectif, analogue ou contraire (186).

The art of suggestion lies sometimes in choosing and setting together words that have rich and multiple associations. This is seen most clearly in the opening line of La Chevelure:

O toison, moutonnant jusque sur l'encolure . . .

The poem evokes the analogy between the waves of his mistress's thick hair, the waves of the sea and his own dreams. From the start, hair and sea come together without transition in 'toison moutonnant'. But by putting these words side by side and leading on to 'encolure' Baudelaire has given several senses at once. 'Moutonnant' normally describes the sea breaking into white-capped waves and has lost its associations with 'mouton'. 'Encolure' can be the shoulder of a human being or the neckline of a dress, but it is also used of the curving neck and withers of a horse. By setting together 'toison', a thick fleece, 'moutonnant' and 'encolure', Baudelaire both intensifies the physical sensation of the luxuriance of the thick hair and the powerful curve of neck and shoulder, and at the same time suggests the associations of a world of rich, primitive animal beauty, to be echoed later in the poem. 'Toison' perhaps also calls up the 'toison d'or' —Jason's pursuit of the golden fleece and so voyages over far seas in search of a magic dream. Even the connecting-words in this line add fully to sense and sound: not simply 'sur' or 'jusqu'à' but 'jusque sur', right down over; this both forms a refrain of *u* sounds leading up to the lovely 'encolure' and emphasises the richness of the flowing waves of hair.

But there is another kind of suggestiveness which is almost the opposite of this rich multiplicity. One of the central problems of art based not on description but on suggestion (Sainte-Beuve saw this in an interesting passage in the *Pensées de Joseph Delorme, XV*) is how to hold the balance between the specific and the general, between the precise and the undefined. Baudelaire sees beauty as 'quelque chose d'un peu vague, laissant carrière à la conjecture' (1255). Suggestion is smothered by over-exact description which leaves no place for the 'lacune complétée par l'imagination de l'auditeur' (1211).[1] Yet if only the most general and undefined words are used, there will be nothing to stimulate or enrich the reader's imagination, which will remain vague and inert.

It is surprising to discover how often Baudelaire uses the most general adjectives: 'charmant', 'étrange', 'vague', 'heureux', 'singulier'. Often their position in the line or in relation to the noun they qualify makes the reader's mind pause over them and call up associations, while set among them are more specific and concrete suggestions. *La Chevelure* might be compared with *Parfum exotique;* their theme is the same, but where *La Chevelure* gives the rich sensuous elaboration, culminating in the 'senteurs confondues De l'huile de coco, du musc et du goudron', *Parfum exotique* moves slowly and dreamily through 'rivages heureux' 'charmants climats', 'arbres singuliers', with just the slight touch of the specific in the scent of the green tamarind trees.

Some of Baudelaire's finest lines fuse fiercely physical and deliberately prosaic images with undefined and abstract terms that suggest infinite prolongations of feeling, and form part of an echoing incantation. In:

> Quand le ciel bas et lourd pèse comme un couvercle
> Sur l'esprit gémissant en proie aux longs ennuis . . . (70)

[1] One is reminded of Mallarmé's remark on one of Zola's novels: 'Tout est dit . . . sans que par une lacune quelconque on puisse y laisser pénétrer de soi ni rêver à côté' (*Propos sur la Poésie*, p. 106).

he moves from the precise, concrete and familiar image, with its hard
consonants forcing home the compression, into the prolonged uncertainty
of 'en proie aux longs ennuis'. In the lines:

> Et les vagues terreurs de ces affreuses nuits
> Qui compriment le cœur comme un papier qu'on froisse (42)

the terrors are utterly undefined; the stressing and lengthening of 'vagues'
and 'affreuses' through the mute *e* make the line stretch into suggestive
distance; then we move into the startling image from the physical world
with the heart being crushed and crumpled like a rejected sheet of paper;
the sounds of 'compriment' and 'froisse' give a sharp sense of pressure
and rustling, and uncertainty contracts into terror.

Constantly Baudelaire fuses abstract and concrete worlds as words from
the one are strangely but aptly fitted to the other:

> Mon âme rêveuse appareille . . . (28)
> Mon esprit subtil que le roulis caresse . . . (25)

He fuses also very different tones; the conversational with the eloquent,
the dignified with the intimate. *Le Cygne* is one of the finest examples.
It moves smoothly and reflectively from the ringing lines that call up
the lovely hieratical gestures of the ancient world where Andromache
weeps, exiled from the river Simoïs, to the anecdote of modern city life,
the swan in the dust and rubble among scavengers' carts at dawn and
the wretched negress exiled in fog and mud. Andromache from the
distant past is made part of an intimate, bare and familiar present in the
direct personal simplicity of the opening: 'Andromaque, je pense à
vous!', while the swan and the negress of the everyday world are given
the dignity of agelong symbols of suffering, revolt and longing:

> Comme les exilés, ridicule et sublime,
> Et rongé d'un desir sans trève . . .

Most suggestive of all is the end. It has been pointed out that Baudelaire
might have chosen to close with a resounding climax as the Parnassians
do:

> Auprès d'un tombeau vide en extase courbée;
> Veuve d'Hector, hélas, et femme d'Hélénus!

Instead, he has moved away gradually from plastic and defined description
through the curtain of mist and the echo of the distant horn, to give in
the simplest words the widest and least defined sense of loss:

> A quiconque a perdu ce qui ne se retrouve
> Jamais, jamais! . . .

and then to fade deliberately and penetratingly into the distance of anonymous and forgotten sorrows:

> Je pense aux matelots oubliés dans une île,
> Aux captifs, aux vaincus! . . . à bien d'autres encor!

Set in Baudelaire's rich evocations of delight or terror there constantly come lines of this piercing simplicity, the strength and bareness of the words brought out by their placing in the rhythm of the single line:

in *Le Balcon*:

> Nous avons dit souvent d'impérissables choses . . .

in *Femmes Damnées*:

> Et cependant je sens ma bouche aller vers toi . . .

in *Le Voyage*:

> Nous nous sommes souvent ennuyés, comme ici . . .

Perhaps only Racine can also give this particular suggestiveness, moving from rich dignity or violence into the sudden stab of the nakedly simple line.

Recueillement (173) gives an impression of extreme simplicity; it shows the delicacy and variety in Baudelaire's art of suggestion at its finest. Valéry has pointed out that there are in this exquisite sonnet three lines dangerously near to the declamatory and the trite (beginning 'Pendant que des mortels . . .') with their awkward inversion, obvious adjectives and perhaps banal image. But in their place in the poem these lines make a burst of angry crudity between the moments of perfect tranquillity at beginning and end; they serve their purpose as a moment of contrast, and the sheer movement of the whole passes without damage across them. In the rest of the poem two very different kinds of suggestion are quietly interwoven; the familiar and intimate in the consolation offered to grief by the everyday, soft, coaxing, repeated words of the child's world ('Sois sage, . . . tiens-toi plus tranquille, . . . donne-moi la main, viens par ici'); and the dignified and majestic in the half-allegorical figures who pass like shadows peopling the background of loneliness— le Soir, le Plaisir, les Années, le Soleil, le Regret, la Nuit. The sonnet evokes vast dimensions of time and space—the dimness round the town, the seething multitudes, the dead years of the past, the depths of the waters, the setting sun on the horizon, the slow trailing approach of night—and against these far-stretching suggestions it sets the sense of closeness and peace. Without perfect balance, the personifications could

have become lofty abstractions, the childhood allusions mere senti-
mentality or triviality: here the solemn and the intimate have been
perfectly fused. There is quiet tenderness in the gently-moving first line
and a breathless waiting in the bare words and split phrasing of the second;
then comes the broadening of rhythm and background as evening falls
over all mankind. Through the long subordinate clause on the crude clan-
gour of the city the lines move quickly back to pick up again the utterly
personal note in tiny phrases giving the withdrawal and the breath of
relief:

> Ma douleur, donne-moi la main, viens par ici
> Loin d'eux.

Then again the vision broadens and imagination touches alive the friendly
phantoms. There is no rich elaboration; simply the slight detail that
transforms abstract allegory into a new meaning as the dead years in
dresses of the past bend closer from high balconies, while from the
depths of the waters regret slowly rises, purified and smiling, and the
setting sun becomes a vagrant falling peacefully asleep under the arch of a
bridge. Depth, space, air, fire and water, the elements and the architecture
of a wide-stretching world are caught together in hieratical gesture and
familiar intimacy, till the child grief sees consolation and rest in terms of
the familiar things of the city: lovely women on lofty balconies or an old
beggar peacefully huddled asleep. In the last two lines the slow and stately
evocation of the advance of night

> Et, comme un long linceul traînant à l'Orient,

moves into the whisper, the pause, the endearment, the hesitation, and
the final flood of relief, again in the simple words of the child's
world:

> Entends, ma chère, entends la douce Nuit qui marche.

The use of sensations to call up feelings and ideas is obviously central
to Baudelaire's art of suggestion. But he is specially original in evoking
sensations less easily definable than those usually classified as visual,
auditory, olfactory and so on: sensations related to basic muscular
or nervous tensions and fundamental rhythms in the human being, which
are only half-realised and rarely analysed in conscious experience, and
reach obsessive force in dream and nightmare. Through them Baudelaire
expresses still more strongly the basic struggle between delight and terror,
aspiration and impotence.

At one extreme there is the sense of stifling: the choking lungs wheeze as they draw in the vitiated city air:

> Et, quand nous respirons, la Mort dans nos poumons
> Descend, fleuve invisible, avec de sourdes plaintes (5);

or the feeling of claustrophobia and contraction as the whole world presses in crushingly:

> Quand le ciel bas et lourd pèse comme un couvercle . . . (70).

The opposite is the feeling of expansion, of breathing and moving freely and joyously:

> La poitrine en avant et les poumons gonflés
> Comme de la toile,
> J'escalade le dos des flots amoncelés (65).

This is pushed to the pitch of ecstatic dream in *Elévation* with its rapturous soaring movement as the weightless body floats effortlessly through outer ether, bathed in coolness, purity and liquid light.

The terror of the seeping away of man's vital substance is a deeply-rooted nightmare experience. Some of Baudelaire's strongest impressions are those of sapping, eating away, undermining, corroding and corrupting, seen at their most intense in *l'Amour et le Crâne* where a grimly charming Cupid blows frail soap-bubbles from the substance of the brain, or in *La Fontaine de Sang* with its endless oozing of blood. In this set of images the world shifts into an insinuating and loathly shapelessness.

But the flux and mobility of things that have no fixed shape can be the emblem of just the opposite. Baudelaire is fascinated by the vast stretches of sea and clouds, shapeless and never still, for they suggest the countless possibilities and patterns which the imagination can form from these fluid elements, and so become the symbol not of decomposition but of creation.

The fascination of fluidity is matched by an equally strong delight in the suggestion of structure. Often Baudelaire transforms the real world by suddenly presenting the most human or the most abstract subject as a set of geometrical shapes. By doing this, he can both play on the instinctive excitement in the discovery of mathematical patterns and relationships, and achieve a particular kind of momentary aesthetic detachment in poems where intense feeling might otherwise become raw, exaggerated or sentimental. When he writes of the skeleton dressed for the ball, the grim reflections on human flesh in its *danse macabre* are both balanced and intensified by his sense of the complex and beautiful structure of the

human framework in itself: 'L'élégance sans nom de l'humaine arma-
ture . . .' In *Les Sept Vieillards* the seven old men are transformed into
sinister diagrams; the spine making a right angle with the legs, another
with the stick, and the stiff beard adding another angle. But it is specially
in *Les Petites Vieilles* that the poet deliberately cuts across pathos and
grandeur as, 'méditant sur la géometrie', he works out the mathematical
problem of how to shape coffins to these distorted bodies. Then, from
the moment of detachment, he moves back, through analogies of
shape, to a tender sense of the likenesses between old age and childhood.

Baudelaire is particularly fascinated by geometrical shapes in movement. The masts and rigging of sailing ships as they sway on the sea
excite him because of

> la multiplication successive et la génération de toutes les courbes et
> figures imaginaires opérées dans l'espace par les éléments réels de
> l'objet; (1261)

they become a symbol of possibility and of creative pattern.

Probably the sensation which gives most rich and varied effects in
Baudelaire's poetry is that of rocking or swaying. It may be the symbol of
delight and creative dreams:

> Et mon esprit subtil que le roulis caresse
> Saura te retrouver, ô féconde paresse!
> Infinis bercements du loisir embaumé! . . (25)

or of indolence and evil:

> Sur l'oreiller du mal c'est Satan Trismégiste
> Qui berce longuement notre esprit enchanté; (5)

it reaches the ecstatic and dream-like in the 'Valse mélancolique et
langoureux vertige' of *Harmonie du Soir*, and becomes the wild tossing of
nightmare at the end of *Les Sept Vieillards*.

Baudelaire's variations on a sense impression may best be seen in *Le
Serpent qui danse*. The centre of the poem is the sensation of sway; sway
which cannot be pinned down and defined but is a vacillation between
two opposing states. This sensation is an essential part of the meaning,
which sways back and forward between the supple indolent beauty and
the hard coldness of the woman, between the ecstasy and the bitterness
of the lover.

The rhythm gives a swaying movement of a particularly strange kind, for it combines the eight-syllabled line not with the familiar six-syllabled one, but with the odd line of five syllables, always seeming to fall short of what we expect and so suggesting an irregular and haunting fascination.

The tiniest details contribute to the impression of swaying, and the poem works in a deliberate crescendo. First Baudelaire evokes impressions of iridescence and fluidity; her skin shimmers like shot silk, calling up the sway between light and shade and the wavering materials as she moves. The scent of her hair sets his dreams sailing on a rocking sea, and suggests both beauty and bitterness by its 'âcres parfums'. Her eyes shimmer with the contradictory suggestions of gold and iron, treasure and harshness. She has the cold, supple attraction of the serpent swaying on the end of a rod; from the tiny shimmer of the start the images have taken on a broader and broader movement, and now the associations of sway with a lazy and fascinating animal beauty reach their climax in the slow dignity of

> Sous le fardeau de ta paresse
> Ta tête d'enfant
> Se balance avec la mollesse
> D'un jeune éléphant . . .

The end of the poem shows how rapidly and subtly Baudelaire moves from one image to another through unexpressed sensuous analogies. As he kisses the woman, 'l'eau de ta bouche' becomes a bitter magic wine, then turns without transition to a liquid sky in which is strewn a burst of stars. Behind the shift in images lies the unexpressed analogy: the stars strew the firmament like tiny bubbles rising and sparkling in wine, and both the sparkle of wine and the burst of stars are like the sudden surge of physical pleasure at the touch of her mouth.

To seize the unexpressed details that link images in this way often adds to the sharpness of their impact. This is particularly so in the terrifying poem *L'Horloge*, with its theme of time sucking away strength. Baudelaire is looking at the hand of a clock; it first suggests a pointed finger threatening. He shifts without transition to the darts of pain quivering in the target of the human heart; the pointed clock-hand has called up the shape of the dart. Then comes the horrible whispering voice of the ticking seconds; tiny and insect-like, it combines with the dart-shapes to suggest the jab of a loathsome mosquito, sucking the life-blood through its sharp proboscis. The associations with draining away then lead on to the image of the water-clock, its tiny relentless droplets trickling time away

as pitilessly as the tick of the seconds or the pricking and sucking of the
minute insect that drains the life-blood.

Baudelaire's notes for a preface to the *Fleurs du Mal* saw versification as
vital among the means of suggestion (186). It is impossible here to
analyse in detail his views on how it is intimately connected both with
what is most abstract and what is most sensuous in man's experience, or
to do more than indicate in the barest way the suppleness with which he
uses the traditional verse forms that are his steady rhythmical ground-
work. A catalogue of different forms is useless unless the reader can feel
how each detail of sound enhances the sense. This is not a dry technical
question, nor music for the sake of music; always sound and pattern are
part of the essential meaning.

Some of the best-known poems create an obsession through the use of
refrain with its incantatory echo, whether lulling and lovely or with the
beat of implacable despair. Litanesque rhythms and repetitions, with all
their associations of dignity and ritual, intensify the compulsive force
and strangeness of feelings often very far from the orthodoxly
religious.

The alexandrine is naturally the most frequent line; Baudelaire gives it
particular richness or lightness through subtle, not over-obvious allitera-
tion, assonance, onomatopoeia and especially the placing of the mute *e*,
but he leaves its basic rhythm strong, clear, dignified and serious; his
sentences may be complex and flow with firm construction over several
lines, but it is only rarely that there is *enjambement* for conversational
tone (parts of *Le Cygne*) or dislocation of the main regular beat (the
displacement of the caesura to underline the desperation of sacrilege in
'Criant à Dieu dans sa furibonde agonie,' in *Le Voyage*).

The eight-syllable line, with its lapidary effect, can give a particular
concentration to the tone of worship (*A la très-chère; Tout entière*) or
to biting despair and hatred (*Le Vampire, L'Irrémédiable*). Alexandrines
interwoven with shorter lines are used in many ways to suggest fluctuat-
ing and indefinable sensations (*Le Poison, L'Irréparable, La Musique*);
often the fall from the alexandrine into the shorter line can intensify the
feeling of disillusion or bitterness. And from the mingling of different
shorter lines Baudelaire creates some of his finest poems. We have seen
the evocative metre of *Le Serpent qui danse*; but the poem that comes
particularly to mind is *L'Invitation au Voyage*, where an even more
haunting effect comes from the use of the odd number of syllables, this

time in lines of five and seven, with the recurring movement from
anticipation into peace as the short line is resolved into the longer:

> Mon enfant, ma sœur,
> Songe à la douceur
> D'aller là-bas vivre ensemble . . .

Neither rhymes nor rhythms, alliterations nor assonances call attention
blatantly to any startling novelty. Baudelaire saw verse as appealing to
'cet amour contradictoire et mystérieux de l'esprit humain pour la
surprise et la symétrie'. He does not dislocate traditional forms but works
his own variations within them. Always it is the combined effect of
sound and sense, of music and meaning that counts, in opening lines
that slowly unfold long vistas:

> Je suis comme le roi d'un pays pluvieux . . . (70)

in echoing refrains:

> Mais le vert paradis des amours enfantines . . . (61)

in heavy assonances with all the weight of weariness:

> *Tant* l'écheveau du *temps lentement* se dévide (31)

or in biting lines that stand out in bare simplicity:

> De n'avoir pas connu ce que pleurent les morts (33).

In his notes for a preface, Baudelaire is deliberately uncompromising
in his conviction that great poetry depends on unremitting effort and that
every detail has behind it 'les retouches, les variantes, les épreuves bar-
bouillées' (1382). The reader who is interested in the stages of creating a
poem might set side by side the first and the final version of *La Mort des
Artistes*, a poem on this very subject, to see how the poet changes images
that are vague and lofty, and expression verging on the flat and trite, to
find a new way of conveying repeated and subtle effort, combined with
self-mockery, in the sharpest and most suggestive terms.

But to see how the slightest detail counts, one need only look at two
tiny alterations in one stanza of *Un Voyage à Cythère* (112). It now reads:

> Ridicule pendu, tes douleurs sont les miennes!
> Je sentis, à l'aspect de tes membres flottants,
> Comme un vomissement, remonter vers mes dents
> Le long fleuve de fiel des douleurs anciennes.

Originally Baudelaire had written:

> Pauvre pendu muet, tes douleurs sont les miennes.

'Pauvre' was too near to sentimental self-pity, and 'muet' was unnecessary; with 'ridicule', in the place of strength before the noun,

Baudelaire calls up what is grotesque, out of place and loathsome in the spectacle, and still applies it as an emblem to himself, intensifying the struggle between disgust and pity for suffering. The last line originally read:

> Le long fleuve de fiel de mes douleurs anciennes.

The change is minute, but in the first reading 'an/ciennes' made only two syllables; by changing 'de mes' into 'des' Baudelaire has been able both to make the grief more general and through the lengthened 'an/ci/ennes' to suggest ancient and p rolonged suffering.

PART II

4. The Outline of the 'Fleurs du Mal'

Baudelaire insisted that the *Fleurs du Mal* was not just a collection of isolated poems but a deliberately arranged sequence, with each poem taking its place in 'un cadre singulier que j'avais choisi'. From birth in *Bénédiction* to death at the end it traces the outline of human destiny, or what Baudelaire once called the 'procession de l'imagination humaine'. Man is searching for some infinite satisfaction, and the poems are grouped to show how he seeks it in turn in art and in love (SPLEEN ET IDEAL), in the life of the city (TABLEAUX PARISIENS), in stimulants (LE VIN), in perversity (FLEURS DU MAL) and in rebellion against the nature of things (LA REVOLTE). The search stems from the will to escape the apathy or the horror provoked by the imperfect nature of the world and the self; it is punctuated by the constant recurrence of lethargy, terror and lucid self-criticism.

This much is immediately obvious. But it is easy to distort the central meaning by presenting the *Fleurs du Mal* as simply recounting a series of escapes that failed. Constantly set against and interwoven with failure, remorse and disgust, there rise the will to struggle, moments of peace and clear-sighted tenderness, pride in what can be salvaged. Some critics see in Baudelaire a repeated movement from aspiration to disillusion. Whether in individual experiences or in the grouping of poems, the movement is more often threefold: first, the reaching out towards a longed-for ecstasy, then the torment of the failure to find perfection, and finally the assertion of the bitter, limited but intense worth that remains. And if the volume leads to its end through a deliberate crescendo of distress, death does not come simply as the emblem of despair, but as one more symbol of man's unquenchable ambitions. The last poem, *Le Voyage*, follows again a threefold movement: threaded first on man's immense desires and then on his sickened disillusionment at 'le spectacle ennuyeux de l'immortel péché', it culminates in the setting sail once again, fired by a bitter but ineradicable hope:

> Nous nous embarquerons sur la mer des Ténèbres
> Avec le cœur joyeux d'un jeune passager . . .

The *Fleurs du Mal* are the intimate epic of the progress of human desire. Desire of three kinds: to enjoy, to understand and to create. Sometimes only the first of these is considered by readers of Baudelaire. But the struggle of the intellect to comprehend the nature and meaning of the self, of others and of the world is equally strong. Baudelaire dedicates his book to the 'âme *curieuse* qui souffre[s]' (163), and the climax of the section LA REVOLTE is man's stretching towards the forbidden tree of the knowledge of good and evil. Then, strongest of all needs is the will to create, to shape the dissatisfaction of experience into the satisfaction of having conquered through expression.

Each of these desires in its search for the absolute finds paradox and suffering. Intense pleasure cannot be timelessly prolonged; man looks for 'de vastes voluptés, *changeantes*, inconnues' (123), and achievement gives way to satiety which intensifies further longing: 'Désir, vieil arbre à qui le plaisir sert d'engrais' (124). The desire for lucid understanding leads to exacerbated and destructive self-analysis, and finds the impossibility of complete understanding between lovers, and the danger of escapism or self-satisfaction in turning to share the lives of others. And in his desire to create, the artist struggles endlessly with apathy and impotence, and is painfully aware how very far expression falls short of intention.

But however virulent and uncompromising their analysis, the *Fleurs du Mal* are not simply the outline of a failure. The moments of ecstasy are the more penetrating because they rise out of and include the lacks and longings of the human condition. The will to understand draws its own tenderness for human beings even from what is imperfect, cruel or grotesque, and finds that the highest courage lies in being able to face evil in the self without the self-indulgence of weak disgust:

> Ah! Seigneur! donnez-moi la force et le courage
> De contempler mon cœur et mon corps sans dégoût! (113)

And the poet knows that from imperfection he has made lasting beauty:

> Tu m'as donné ta boue et j'en ai fait de l'or. (180)

5. *Au Lecteur*

The book opens with a challenge. The reader is to share the poet's experience not through admiration for a superior figure, not through pity for an inferior, not in any comforting complicity; he is the

> Hypocrite lecteur, mon semblable, mon frère.

Even the sins we have not committed are latent in us, avoided from cowardice, not virtue. And at the root of evil lies *l'Ennui*, that world-weariness that rots away will-power, sinks into perverse dreams or stimulates the desperate snatching at forbidden pleasures.

Au Lecteur is deliberately rhetorical in its unalleviated intensity, and firmly constructed to lead through a series of shocks to its final stab. There are moments of over-declamatory violence and forced effect, and the final picture of *l'Ennui* is too close to the bric-à-brac appurtenances of romantic fashion. But its best stanzas choose words and images with an extraordinary richness of undertone to convey how man is eaten away by vices which are at once loathsome, insinuating and cherished. The central impression is of seething and sapping corruption, but each sense is called into play as man is rocked on a soft pillow, or transmuted into a wisp of vapour, plods downward through stinking shadows or is jerked like a puppet on a string. His seeming remorse is weak and nauseous self-indulgence: the expression 'nous nous faisons payer *grassement* nos aveux' suggests as well as the rich reward the unctuous satisfaction. The hidden skill of the forces that prey on the will comes alive in the subtle inverted alchemy of Satan and in *Ennui* as 'ce monstre *délicat*'—hypercritical, fastidious and dextrous.

The opening poem has shown the destructive forces at work within man: the first group of poems turns to the struggle of the will to create.

6. *Spleen et Idéal*

The Poems on Art

The first twenty-one poems are all related, directly or indirectly, to Baudelaire's ideas on the problems of the artist and the nature of beauty. They are deliberately arranged to start from the more conventionally romantic attitude (the persecution and the mission of the poet as seen in *Bénédiction* and *L'Albatros*), then gradually to introduce the different qualities which Baudelaire associates with his personal conception of beauty, as he develops it in *Fusées* (X) (1255), and to lead up to a challenging climax in the *Hymne à la Beauté*.

Poems on the role of the poet and the writing of poetry are often important in the history of literary movements rather than being great poems in themselves. This section of the *Fleurs du Mal* is interesting mainly because it suggests themes that are to be developed during the rest of the book; with one or two outstanding exceptions, these are not

Baudelaire's finest poems, though they contain many lovely lines or
stanzas.

Bénédiction and *L'Albatros* form a general introduction. They show the
poet as the romantics saw him, an innocent victim exiled in society. Perhaps because the theme is familiar and the development simple, they
have become two of the most popular anthology poems of Baudelaire.
They have the firm dignity of good oratory, and *Bénédiction*, sometimes
forced or clumsy, reaches suggestive beauty in moments of litanesque
incantation or sudden simplicity (especially in the speech of the woman)
and in the image at the end where the rhetoric dies out and the vision of
Paradise turns to the shining of its splendour in the dimmed mirror of
the human eye.

Elévation and *Correspondances* give the poet's vision of ecstasy. Instead
of asserting in abstract and intellectual terms a Mission as a Thinker, they
convey physically a complex enhancement of the sense of delight,
mystery and pattern in the world. (See above, pp. 20–2 and 27.)

Ecstasy gives way to a group of poems on the artist's struggles and
sufferings. In *J'aime le souvenir*, seeing the ugliness of the modern world,
he is tempted to turn to ancient beauty, as the Parnassians were to do; yet
in this ugliness there are to be found 'des beautés inconnues'. *Les Phares*
is worth special study as a subtle evocation of the spirit of eight great
artists seen through Baudelaire's individual sensibility; their works are
linked together as expressions of man's restless longings and his wretched-
ness, but the artist's expression of these desires and sufferings bears
witness to man's pride and dignity—there is no sentimental religiosity in
the last stanza, but a suggestion that will lead on to the section LA
REVOLTE. The next five poems call up in various forms the difficulties
faced by the artist; by far the finest is *L'Ennemi*, with its echoing terror
as unused time eats away at man:

> O douleur! ô douleur! Le Temps mange la vie,
> Et l'obscur Ennemi qui nous ronge le cœur
> Du sang que nous perdons croît et se fortifie!

Beauty as Baudelaire saw it was 'quelque chose d'ardent et de triste,
quelque chose d'un peu vague, laissant carrière à la conjecture' (1255).
The next three poems (*La Vie antérieure, Bohémiens en Voyage, L'Homme
et la Mer*) suggest this fusion of longing and loveliness, restlessness and
mystery; the first eight lines of *La Vie antérieure* are one of Baudelaire's
finest evocations of the immensity, the solemnity and the richness of a
strange dream-world.

In his definition of beauty Baudelaire also included 'des ambitions ténébreusement refoulées . . . quelquefois l'idée d'une insensibilité vengeresse' (1255). So he has placed here two poems on human pride and its defiance of all the forces behind the universe. In *Don Juan* it has a half-cruel and half-admirable dignity; in *Châtiment de l'Orgueil* it is pushed to its paroxysm in man's wish to rival the Creator, and leads, as would all achievement of the absolute, to self-destruction.

La Beauté has often been called a Parnassian poem, hymning a statuesque beauty out of keeping with Baudelaire's other theories; too much has been made of this. The central theme is that of the distance that separates man from his ideal; as in the love poems, the figure of a cold and lovely goddess calls up the fascination and the impossibility in the pursuit of perfection. And the poem ends not with the plastic and the statuesque, but with the suggestion typical of Baudelaire: the sense of the fluid and unfathomable in the depths of the human eye.

Baudelaire once remarked 'le beau est toujours bizarre' (956), and in *L'Idéal* and *La Géante* he expresses the fascination of the excessive, with occasional lovely lines of sensuous discovery.

The two concluding poems come back to Baudelaire's basic sense of complexity and conflict. In *Le Masque*, beneath apparent serenity there lies atrocious suffering, and the last lines, simple and knell-like, recall that deadly weariness from which the volume set out:

> C'est que demain, hélas! il faudra vivre encore!
> Demain, après-demain et toujours!—comme nous!

and so lead up to *Hymne à la Beauté*, which ends this group with a provocation. The deliberately lofty rhetorical tone is in keeping with the desperation which, far from denying, asserts and then struggles to ignore moral values. Sometimes trite or crude in expression, but with moments of subtly suggestive image:

> Le Destin charmé suit tes jupons comme un chien . . .,

the poem at the same time underscores the destruction inherent in the pursuit of intensity:

> L'éphémère ébloui vole vers toi, chandelle,
> Crépite, flambe et dit: Bénissons ce flambeau!
> L'amoureux pantelant incliné sur sa belle
> A l'air d'un moribond caressant son tombeau,

and accepts it with all its dangers:

> Qu'importe, si tu rends . . .
> L'univers moins hideux et les instants moins lourds?

The Love Poems

The love poems fall into three main groups, associated with the names of three women. Sometimes a poem originally addressed to one woman may have been transferred to another. It is not details about the real women that matter to our understanding (see pp. 61–2) but the fact that in the *Fleurs du Mal* Baudelaire deliberately arranged the poems to show three very different kinds of love, each with its own atmosphere, and that within each group there is an equally intentional sequence of meaning.

Numbers 22 to 39 (*Parfum exotique* to *Je te donne ces vers*) are the poems to Jeanne Duval; these evoke physical passion, placed first perhaps as the instinctive force that draws man to woman. Here the lover is obsessed by the sensuous beauty of a woman who has not the qualities of mind or heart to bring unity in understanding. Numbers 40 to 48 (*Semper Eadem* to *Le Flacon*), to Madame Sabatier, seem to move to the opposite extreme; this is the love that sets its idol on a pedestal and worships her as an intangible ideal. Numbers 49 to 57 (*Le Poison* to *A une Madone*), to Marie Daubrun, express the complex feeling of the man who knows that youth is past, that passion means suffering, and yet is once more obsessed, with the intensified cruelty and the increased tenderness of an ageing love.

There is neither detailed physical description nor developed abstract analysis of the character of the loved woman. Baudelaire takes only a few features—her hair, her scent, her swaying walk or her eyes—to start resonances in his own feelings. Not herself, but the dreams and struggles she provokes in him are the main centre. But suggestions and images evoke richly three very different experiences of love associated with three different personalities, as each woman calls up in the lover's mind a 'pays qui te ressemble'.

In the first cycle, physical love and the dark mistress Jeanne Duval are associated with dreams of rich, exotic, immensely distant lands, with tropical heat and languor, or with the primitive, instinctive, unreflecting and cruel beauty of the animal world; words, images and rhythms convey a sensuous and supple majesty. The idealism of the Madame Sabatier poems uses religious imagery—church candles, incense, the monstrance and the Host—and the rhythms are light and ethereal or litanesque in keeping with religious adoration. For the love of maturity he has chosen associations with Dutch paintings and the landscape of the Low Countries, and with a background of autumn; when his imagination sets sail it is not now for tropical seas but for the mist-wreathed canals of a land that is half-familiar, half-exotic, as love has become a repeated but a constantly new experience. The calm and comfort of the rooms and furnishings of the rich merchant country to which the ships return from tropical voyages echo the longing for a quiet, mature, experienced and comforting tenderness after the fierce ambitions of the past.

Within these three very different groups, the poems are deliberately arranged to follow the same sequence of experience. The first poem in each cycle suggests both fascination and danger. Then come the poems of ecstasy. Gradually all the forces of insufficiency and stress, cruelty and remorse rise to a pitch of tormented hatred. But in each group this is followed by a moment of renewed and intense tenderness, growing out of a shared past and the acceptance of sorrow or imperfection. Finally there comes the virulent yet triumphant assertion of the bitter beauty that can be salvaged and preserved, for two forces conquer despair, disgust and the ravages caused by time or human folly: memory, and the art of expressing what memory holds.

It has become fashionable to talk of the lack of contact between lovers in Baudelaire's poems, and a good deal of misplaced ingenuity has been devoted to presenting them as monuments of sterile contemplation or symbols of sexual impotence. It is true that for Baudelaire woman is one of many ways of suggesting both the wonder and the terror in the desire for what is out of reach, and intensity of desire may often be brought out more strongly in longing than in fulfilment. But if sometimes Baudelaire places woman at an uncapturable distance, yet many of the poems are quite plainly written to express full physical possession, whether they evoke the rising violence of passion or the languid and melancholy tenderness that follows satisfaction. For the pursuit of the unattainable can also be suggested by the sequence of fulfilment, satiety, weariness and renewed longing.

To Baudelaire man and woman are indeed frighteningly separate, but this sense of isolation even in moments of closest approach to another human being is a good deal more subtle than a mere refusal of physical satisfaction. In fact, its full bitterness may come from the contrast between physical closeness and the impossibility of sharing thought or feeling. And, on the other hand, out of the feeling of separation he draws some of his most extraordinary moments of precarious peace.

In expressing physical passion, Baudelaire is in turn specific and allusive, forthright and stylised. He can show its crudity and its beauty, its cruelty and its tenderness. The condemnation of certain poems in 1857 as pornographic, and many discussions of them since, have perhaps missed one central thing. The pornographic author makes of the sexual act something shabby and impoverished; through his treatment it becomes spicy, mechanical and essentially trivial, a means of sneering at human behaviour. Baudelaire shows its full complexity, but in the balance of beauty and terror, sympathy and judgment on which he constantly plays, he leaves human dignity completely intact.

If we look now at the poems in their order, we shall see more clearly how they express, in three different tones, the same sequence of experience: first, the dreams of delight, then the torment, and finally the recognition, through memory and art, of the imperfect, bitter and fallible, but intensely human worth of what the experience has meant.

First, the poems to Jeanne. Physical love is the central theme; the woman has a supple, thoughtless animal loveliness, and the stimulus of a purely physical sophistication. The poem which originally opened the group, *Les Bijoux*, is now to be found in *Les Epaves*. This is the introduction to the theme of desire, and beneath the slow, reflective and musical evocation of the beauty of the naked body, the suggestions of disturbance, danger and cruelty are implicit in many of the images, leading up to the flicker of blood-red firelight at the close. Delight and threat are suggested from the outset.

Parfum exotique and *La Chevelure* are the poems of ecstasy. Their abstract meaning is the mingling of stimulus and peace, but this is woven entirely through suggestive sense-impressions. The imagination is set sailing over distant tropical seas, to lands where mankind is primitive and vigorous, or rocked on gentle waves as the ships lie in the safety of the harbour.

We have already seen (p. 22) the multiplicity of associations crowding behind even the first line of *La Chevelure*, one of the most subtly suggestive of all Baudelaire's poems. It moves back and forth between the dream of the distant seas and the sensuous reality of the thick tresses, evoking each in terms of the other. Setting out from the dim, enclosed and sheltering room, it expands into its climax of ecstatic adventure in the third and fourth stanzas with their dazzling light and tropical heat, proud ships in resounding ports and iridescent sea of shimmering gold and shot-silk; the echo of the heavy sounds *a, oi, â*, intensifies the richness:

> Où les vaisseaux, glissant dans l'or et dans la moire,
> Ouvrent leurs vastes bras pour embrasser la gloire
> D'un ciel pur ou frémit l'éternelle chaleur.

Then it falls back into the sense of peace and shelter, leading up to one of Baudelaire's loveliest images, impossible to paraphrase and depending on the immediacy and simultaneity of associations:

> Cheveux bleus, pavillon de ténèbres tendues,
> Vous me rendez l'azur du ciel immense et rond . . .

Her hair suggests infinite desire and delight, and so the infinity of blue in sea and sky; it is jet-black hair with a blue sheen; it shelters him like a tent, the taut stretch of canvas and its shelter conveyed in 'tendues', and the protective shadows and the darkness of the hair in 'ténèbres': these associations can be picked out separately, but only the lines as Baudelaire wrote them will give the full richness of the 'sorcellerie évocatoire'.

Thirteen poems (if we include *Le Léthé* from *Les Epaves*) now turn to the complexities and sufferings of love. This is love for a woman both skilled and insatiable in physical pleasure (*Tu mettrais l'univers, Sed non satiata*), but without emotion or understanding (the end of *Une nuit que j'étais; Remords posthume; Le Léthé*). Baudelaire can convey at the same time the virulent and exasperated crudity of a desperate physical desire and a deliberately formalised ceremonial, delicate or dignified. He does this especially in *Je t'adore à l'égal* . . . and in *Sed non satiata* (a poem often strangely misinterpreted), where the lovely second stanza leads into the age-old complaint of woman's sexual greed as impossible to satisfy, but evokes it through an elaborate tissue of classical allusions.

Two of these poems in particular should be looked at more closely. First, *Une Charogne*. It is not just a brilliant piece of macabre elaboration but is constructed to lead up to the last two lines:

> . . . j'ai gardé la forme et l'essence divine
> De mes amours décomposés!

This again is an age-old theme: the artist through memory and expression can conquer age, decay and death. Baudelaire's originality appears in two main ways. The real cruelty of the poem lies less in its revolting picture of decomposition than in its attitude to the woman, brought home by the fusing of discrepant tones: side by side with the ironical, graceful, half-archaic and courtly terms of worship: 'mon âme', 'la reine des grâces', 'mon ange et ma passion', the formal 'vous' and the lofty musical past historic (not: 'tu t'es presque évanouie' but 'vous crûtes vous évanouir') are set the crude and violent 'puanteur' and the analogy between the position of the decaying animal and the body of the woman in physical passion. For the nature of the woman here spoken to is the same as in two prose poems, *La Femme Sauvage et la Petite Maîtresse*, and *Les Yeux des Pauvres* (241, 268); she is the frivolous and feelingless creature who cannot face up to suffering and horror, and this is the effort to shock her into seeing reality.

Still more important is the way in which each physical detail of disgust has been made gradually, almost imperceptibly but extremely suggestively, to contribute not just to horror but to victory. The decaying body becomes a heap of seething particles, forced on all the senses by their thick ooze, loathly movement and the sound of buzzing flies. But slowly each of these sense-impressions takes its place in a pattern of loveliness. And this is not ingenious aestheticism but part of the essential meaning. The end of the poem is no sudden switch in feeling; it has been working out slowly in the implications of the imagery:

Et ce monde rendait une étrange musique
    Comme l'eau courante et le vent
Ou le grain qu'un vanneur d'un mouvement rhythmique
    Agite et tourne dans son van.

Corruption has been made to evoke the cleanliness of water and the freshness of wind, the thick liquid has moved into the transparent and the ethereal, and the seething particles become the swirl of grain in the winnowing sieve, with the associations of sifting the wheat from the chaff and the winnowing of the souls in death. And the disappearance of shape into formlessness is followed by the image of the artist gradually shaping the dimness of memory into beautiful form.

To Baudelaire, conquest of terror and decay can come only if the full disgust has been faced and expressed. This is no gentle Ronsardian stylisation of death, but it is far from being simply shock for shock's sake. The poem has a cruel and bitter originality, but its tiniest details assert, over decay and destruction, the victory of memory and creation.

Remords posthume evokes in a different way the threat of death. Here the sense-impressions stress the contrast between soft and lovely human flesh and the cold tomb; words and rhythm call up careless grace, indolent and supple sensuousness, gay dancing walk and wilful adventurousness; these spirited and delicate qualities will find in death not the lofty 'alcôve' and 'manoir' with their associations of comfort, sensuality, safety and warmth; instead each word calls up the weight of the marble monument (la pierre opprimant ta poitrine peureuse), the vault into which the rain seeps, and the brutal bareness of the 'fosse creuse', all leading up to the deadly simple line, addressed to the woman who has not known the real worth of life while she lived:

Que vous sert . . .
De n'avoir pas connu ce que pleurent les morts?

Throughout the other poems of this section the sense of being obsessed by a cruel and pitiless beauty increases, to reach its pitch of hatred in the over-declamatory *Duellum*. Then comes the moment of reconciliation, intensely tender in *Le Balcon*, passionate and bitter in *Le Possédé*. *Le Balcon* creates the moment of rich peace as the lovers recall all that has held them together in the past. The refrain, winding in and out like an incantation from the soft echoes of the opening: '*Mère des souvenirs, maîtresse des maîtresses*', lulls and rocks them. Tenderness, rest, companionship, safety, seclusion: these are abstracts, but Baudelaire creates them through physical things: firelight, misty evenings, his eyes searching for hers in the shadows, the protective caress of his hand on her feet as she falls asleep. The first poems to Jeanne had moved from the fireside and the sheltering room outwards into immense adventure; now vast space narrows in until they are shut in safety by shadows: 'La nuit s'épaississait ainsi qu'une cloison' . . . To the abstract idea that the enchantment of the past may be reborn, Baudelaire gives the image of the sun rising to a new day as if washed in the depths of the sea: the whole poem suggests both stretching space and close intimacy. This is the odd, frail and intense peace that comes from knowing imperfection (Car à quoi bon chercher . . .) yet accepting shared memories in a deep tenderness.

Two poems close the Jeanne cycle by calling together beauty and bitterness, destruction and the final triumph. In *Un Fantôme*, around an at first insubstantial ghost he re-creates all the sense-impressions of the previous poems: her careless, childlike, sensuous animal beauty, her scent, her heavy supple hair, her jewels, the richly flowing stuffs which caressed her body, until he has 'dans le présent le passé restauré'. That past has been reduced to ashes, worn away by disease and death; yet the final words cast their biting challenge to time:

Tu ne tueras jamais dans ma mémoire
Celle qui fut mon plaisir et ma gloire!

Je te donne ces vers again recalls her beauty and coldness, knows that to others she seems worthless, and yet creates the poem that will beat like an obsession through the ages, carrying her memory to the future. It has a

magnificent opening, recalling the proud *Exegi monumentum* of Horace
or Ronsard's 'Afin qu'à tout jamais de siècle en siècle vive . . .', and
leads through the long deliberate dignity of the first six lines to the
climax of its drum-beat

> Afin que . . .
> Ta mémoire, pareille aux fables incertaines,
> Fatigue le lecteur ainsi qu'un tympanon. . . .

The poems to Jeanne have called up a woman whose every movement
delights the senses, who has the beauty, the candour and the cruelty of
the thoughtless primitive creature; and through her the experience of
ecstasy, bitterness, sudden intense peace and the survival of memory and
art. *Semper Eadem* opens the cycle to Madame Sabatier; the title itself
shows that in this very different love the same central feelings will be
seen. The first poem again suggests both fascination and threat; from the
beginning he knows that she is merely the pretext for a lovely and con-
soling dream. This time the central quality evoked in the woman is her
gaicty ('votre joie, éclatante pour tous', 'ange plein de gaieté', 'celle qui est
trop gaie'); she stands for natural health and joy. Instead of the rich and
sensual associations of the tropical or the animal world, everything here
suggests purity and grace. In the opening poem to Jeanne, it was her
thick, scented hair that protected his dreams; here it is the delicate and
graceful eyelashes that become the symbol of shelter in the gentle
incantatory invocation:

> Laissez, laissez mon cœur s'enivrer d'un *mensonge*,
> Plonger dans vos beaux yeux comme dans un beau songe,
> Et sommeiller longtemps à l'ombre de vos cils!

The poems of ecstasy that follow play on the terms of religious adoration: 'dictame', 'métamorphose mystique', 'chair spirituelle', 'clarté mystique', and the solemn litany of ritual, worshipping 'la très-belle, la
très-bonne, la très-chère', 'l'Ange gardien, la Muse et la Madone'.

After the poems of delight, feelings again grow complex and bitter.
Man's conflicting instincts drive him to worship the ideal and yet to hate
it for being so different from what he himself is. And it is in this apparently
idyllic cycle that the poems of the most insinuating cruelty and sinister
despair are found. *A Celle qui est trop gaie* (now in *Les Epaves*) creates the
dream landscape that mirrors her—one of cool winds, clear skies and
dancing flowers—then turns to the virulent desire to destroy that gaiety
and natural health which are so insulting a contrast to his own weariness

and corruption. *Réversibilité*, beneath the litany hymning her per-fections ('Ange plein de gaieté, bonté, santé, beauté, bonheur, joie et lumières') has many bitter undertones: first, in the paradoxical im-perfection of her perfect qualities, for how can she understand or share in suffering; then in the threat of what she will come to know when later, ageing and wrinkled, she looks into eyes that express only 'la secrète horreur du dévouement'; finally in the twist at the end where he asks for no ordinary love but leaves her set on her distant pedestal.

In *Confession* the imagined goddess destroys herself; instead of shining in her 'radieuse gaieté' she becomes a harsh and plaintive voice horribly whispering of her own hard lot and of the mechanical tricks of the trade hidden behind the façade of the gay and lovely woman. The contrast between the flooding light of the full moon and the sinister streets with their shadows of creeping cats, the rhythm with its fall from long to short line, the style moving from dignified to flatly conversational, all bring out the intimacy and the horror of disillusion as the idol becomes no more than a trite and plaintive woman.

Yet the dream of her still follows him as the contrast to lust or wretched-ness; *L'Aube spirituelle* in this group takes the same theme as *Une nuit que j'étais* . . . in the Jeanne cycle, but in a very different tone.

Harmonie du Soir is, like *Le Balcon* for Jeanne, the moment of intense peace drawn from the sorrow and beauty of memories. In both there is a background of sunset and of mist, and a twining, lulling refrain, but here there is no evocation of physical love; memories are called up by the most delicate of the sensations—flower-scents, the quavering note of the violin—and by religious imagery: scent like incense, the sky a flower-decked altar, the shape of the setting sun like the Communion Host, till memory shines as from a holy monstrance.

The cycle closes with *Le Flacon*, a grim assertion of the power of memory. Whatever he may become through pain, age or disease, he will hold the ineradicable memory of the delight and suffering she pro-voked. Again it is not her physical qualities that the poem recalls, as *Un Fantôme* had done for Jeanne; the memory of her is symbolised by the delicate gauzy wings of the butterfly bursting from the chrysalis, the religious allusion to Lazarus rising from the tomb, and the intangible persistent perfume that lingers in the empty dusty bottle.

The poems of the third group, to Marie Daubrun, show a love con-scious of age and weariness, and with a particular tone of mature and complex tenderness. The woman evoked here is mysterious and ambiguous, 'enchanteresse' and 'sorcière'. We see particularly her strange eyes; Jeanne's eyes had been cold and empty, Madame Sabatier's seemed to hold a mystic light; these are eyes of subtle changing colours and move constantly between tears and laughter.

The two opening poems, *Le Poison* and *Ciel Brouillé*, suggest, like *Les Bijoux* and *Semper Eadem* in the previous groups, but through different images, the sense of magic and threat implicit in love. *Ciel Brouillé* is one of the subtlest of Baudelaire's evocations of a woman, a countryside and his own inner struggles each in terms of the other. The changing shades in her eyes reflect moods of tenderness, dreaminess or cruelty; they call up a misty autumn countryside with sudden gleams of sun, and this echoes the mood of the poet when the intellect is sunk in a mist of lethargy and the restless nerves flash their need to escape:

> Tu rappelles ces jours blancs, tièdes et voilés,
> Qui font se fondre en pleurs les cœurs ensorcelés,
> Quand, agités d'un mal inconnu qui les tord,
> Les nerfs trop éveillés raillent l'esprit qui dort.

And finally, the sunset through the autumn mists suggests the winter to come, holding sharp unknown pleasures, as may this new love at the approach of age.

The poems of ecstasy follow. In the Jeanne cycle there had been a poem on cats which evoked sensuality and cruelty; the cat poem to Marie calls on quite different suggestions—the penetrating and ambiguous sound of its voice, now light and tender, now rich and deep, and the fascination of strange, opaline, gleaming eyes.

He finds in her a rich and opulent beauty, strangely combined with something childlike, and the echoing refrain in *Le Beau Navire* sways between the two sides to her loveliness:

> Je veux te peindre ta beauté,
> Où l'enfance s'allie à la maturité . . .
> D'un air placide et triomphant
> Tu passes ton chemin, majestueuse enfant . . .

The need to be protected and to protect are interwoven; she is not the passion or the idol, but 'enfant', 'sœur' or 'mère'. In *L'Invitation au Voyage* the incantation is not that of heavy sensuous languor nor of triumphant hymnody, but the slow, rich, ordered peace of

> Là, tout n'est qu'ordre et beauté,
> Luxe, calme et volupté.

The ships return with the spoils of the east to the mist-wreathed canals of the Low Countries, the 'pays qui te ressemble'; and the secrecy and promise of love, enriched by a prolonged past, is suggested by the shining comfort, the patina and polish of rooms and furniture: 'armoire à doux secrets, pleine de bonnes choses', or

> Des meubles luisants,
> Polis par les ans,
> Décoreraient notre chambre . . .
> Les riches plafonds,
> Les miroirs profonds . . .

Of all Baudelaire's poems of delight, *L'Invitation au Voyage* is perhaps the most subtle and the most mature.

Ecstasy is again followed by suffering. In *L'Irréparable* he cries out from inescapable gnawing destruction, not to the cold goddess or the angelic idol, but, in keeping with Marie Daubrun the actress, to the traditional sorceress or fairy who at the end of the pantomime strikes down the forces of evil—but for whom he waits endlessly in vain. And in *Causerie* the sequence of desire and destruction continues.

The tender acceptance of what remains comes with *Chant d'Automne*. In the first half the sound of logs thudding on the cobbles in autumn calls up through linked sense-impressions anguish, oppression and a desperate sense of passing time. Obsessed by this echoing sound and by the coming winter which it suggests, 'bercé par ce choc monotone', he turns to find the moment of intense fleeting peace, and the metre leads into a renewed rocking movement:

> Et pourtant, aimez-moi, tendre cœur! soyez *mère*,
> *Mê*me pour un ingrat, *même* pour un méchant;
> Amante ou sœur, soyez la douceur éphé*mère*
> D'un glorieux automne ou d'un soleil couchant . . .

The farewell poem of this cycle, *A une Madone*, is the cruellest of all. Its general meaning is still the same as in the poems that end the other groups: out of beauty and torment, a lasting memory will be preserved —here symbolised by the altar which he will lovingly construct for her, and on which he will then sadistically sacrifice her. It is a piece of elaborately embroidered artifice. Baudelaire has taken the most raw and corrosive human emotion, jealousy, and, echoing the need in this worst humiliation to prove that intellectual command remains, has developed it in the most deliberately stylised conceits. This is a hyper-subtle poem, with a touch of the decadent in its over-ingenuity and its violent conclusion. But there is extreme skill in the way in which the creation of the stiff, rigid, barbaric image, heavy robes and jewelled surface is made to encase a terrible tenderness and set against the fluid, mobile, menacing and undefined spirit of desire.

At the end of the three main groups Baudelaire has placed a few miscellaneous love poems. The finest are *Moesta et Errabunda* with its delicate refrain calling up the world of childhood, and *Sonnet d'Automne* with its weary gentleness.

The love poems have traced the interweaving of fascination and fear, delight and anguish, loneliness, hatred and tenderness, intense momentary peace and the final bitter defiance to time and change, the challenge offered by memory and creation.

Spleen

Through *Les Hiboux*, the reproach to man's restlessness, and *La Pipe*, the emblem of his indolence, Baudelaire moves from rocking dreams at the beginning of *La Musique* to reach the

> . . . calme plat, grand miroir
> De mon désespoir.

World-weariness was a frequent enough theme in the century, but Baudelaire's *Spleen* is very different from stock romantic *ennui*. It is neither abstract nor complacent. Weariness and dissatisfaction no longer parade as proofs of superiority; the longing for death is shown with all the undertones of ugliness and disgust (*Le Mort joyeux*), and even clear-sightedness in criticising the self is exposed as a satanic stimulus to further pride. But above all, when Baudelaire conveys the restlessness and the indolence which combine in the world of *spleen*, it is through the objects of the everyday world that grate on the nerves, and through the sense of stifling lethargy or tearing nervous tension, of claustrophobic terror or dreary emptiness. His soul is like a cracked bell, a moonless graveyard, a ship caught in the frightening loveliness of polar ice; he longs for total night but the stars become thousands of watchful eyes to haunt him; the malevolent ticking of the clock whispers its hideous message of the wasting away of life.

These are poems that often open with a trailing and suggestive line:

> Je suis comme le roi d'un pays pluvieux . . .
> J'ai plus de souvenirs que si j'avais mille ans . . .

They bring alive in thudding monosyllables the bare desire for sheer nothingness:

> Car je cherche le vide, et le noir, et le nu . . .

or prolong endlessly the slow passing of fruitless time:

> Rien n'égale en longueur les boiteuses journées,
> Quand sous les lourds flocons des neigeuses années
> L'ennui, fruit de la morne incuriosité,
> Prend les proportions de l'immortalité.

They reach their most obsessive in the brief, almost breathless lines of *L'Héautontimorouménos* and *L'Irrémédiable*, with the terror of being trapped in self-contemplation and self-destruction, and in *L'Horloge* (see p. 29).

One of the best is the *Spleen* poem beginning '*Pluviôse, irrité* . . .' This opens with an allegorical figure brought alive in a new and suggestive way. Pluviôse, the name in the old revolutionary calendar for January–February, stands as a stylised figure pouring water from an urn; at the same time the sound and associations of the word evoke a dismal season of rains and an outmoded past, while 'irrité' suggests the central mood of the poem, and the personification leads into the obsessive coming alive of every object. The hieratical gesture of the allegorical figure and the stretch of city and graveyard, with dead and living plunged in dank discomfort, narrow into a room with its everyday objects. There is no statement or analysis of mood; simply the skinny and mangy cat prowls, seeking vainly for rest and comfort on the hard tiled floor, while the wailing of a cat on the roof seems like the ghost of a dead poet; by movement, sound, touch, shape, the shudder of disgust and of cold ('galeux' and 'frileux'), exasperation and discomfort have been roused in all the senses. The words at the same time convey the real sounds of tolling bell, hissing log and wheezing clock, and give them a menacing and miserable personality:

> Le bourdon se lamente, et la bûche enfumée
> Accompagne en fausset la pendule enrhumée.

Finally the poem contracts still further, and instead of an open lament for a lost past, there is just a pack of cards with their smell of dirt, inherited from a dropsical old woman; they too grate on the senses and come sinisterly alive, as the Knave of Hearts and Queen of Spades chat grimly over their lost love affairs, with the deliberate thud in the final sound:

> Le beau valet de cœur et la reine de pique
> Causent sinistrement de leurs amours défunts.

D

The complex feelings inherent in nervous tension (see p. 16) have been created through their everyday physical equivalents.

Even *spleen* is two-sided, not simply an experience of horror ('Il est amer et doux, pendant les nuits d'hiver . . .'). And one quality, with all its greatness and all its danger, refuses to give in, and points forward to the rest of the book:

> Un phare ironique, infernal,
> Flambeau des grâces sataniques,
> Soulagement et gloire uniques,
> —La conscience dans le Mal!

7. *Tableaux Parisiens*

In one of Baudelaire's prose poems, *Les Fenêtres*, he wanders through the streets at night, gazing in at candle-lit windows, imagining the lives led by the people he sees for a brief moment, and comes home 'fier d'avoir vécu et souffert dans d'autres que moi-même'. Perhaps, he says, the reader will ask whether what he imagined of their lives was true, and he replies:

> Qu'importe ce que peut être la réalité placée hors de moi, si elle m'a aidé à vivre, à sentir que je suis et ce que je suis? (288)

The outer world is there not simply to be described, but as a stimulus to the appetites of the imagination and an instrument of self-analysis.

Several poems show the imagination at work on reality. *Paysage* transforms chimney-pots and drain-pipes seen from a garret into the masts and rigging of ships, and calls up in winter an imagined spring. The sun becomes the emblem of the poet hobbling and poking over cobbles and into corners until every dullest object is changed by his touch. In *A une Mendiante rousse* he imagines the beggar-girl as she would look in sixteenth-century court costume, and in *Rêve parisien* creates a dream city from metals and minerals.

But poetry must contain 'le monde extérieur à l'artiste' as well as 'l'artiste lui-meme'. Even in the poems that most transform the real world, Baudelaire sharpens the outlines of that world as it is; *Paysage* starts from the Paris workshops, the lamplit windows and thick coal-smoke; the beggar-girl is at the end stripped of her imagined adornments and stands skinny and freckled:

> sans autre ornement
> Que ta maigre nudité,
> O ma beauté!

These are no poems of sentimental pity for the poor and the outcast. In his prose works Baudelaire lucidly attacks as a temptation 'le dilettantisme dans la charité' (413), 'la prostitution fraternitaire', that pharisaical pride in pity which may be 'le premier germe de l'esprit satanique' (379). Instead of drawing sickly pathos from lofty or innocent victims, he brings alive all that is grotesque or even loathsome in his subjects, associates them with his own struggles, and suggests the complex attraction that draws him to them, a combination of self-indulgence, compassion and creative pride. In all experience (the love-poems have already shown this) man seeks alternately to lose and to intensify his individual consciousness; so here he may turn to escape in a 'bain de multitude' (243, 414) or to pride in multiplying his appetite for imagined experience, living the lives of the little old women:

> Je goûte à votre insu des plaisirs clandestins . .
> Sombres ou lumineux, je vis vos jours perdus;
> Mon cœur multiplié jouit de tous vos vices!
> Mon âme resplendit de toutes vos vertus!

Precisely because he spares neither his subjects nor himself, involvement becomes genuine.

The three finest poems in this section are Le Cygne (see p. 24), Les Sept Vieillards and Les Petites Vieilles. The two poems of old age and poverty form a deliberate contrast. Les Sept Vieillards is the poem of the threat and terror of the outer world. Every detail in the opening picture of the city gives a feeling of contraction and nightmare: it swarms as with tiny ants; the streets are narrow canals in which mystery is pent like sap; a dirty yellow fog blankets things; carts roll by like tumbrils and ghosts seem to accost the passer-by. The poet, every sinew stiff with apprehension, stays motionless as the ominous procession of strange old men goes by, then rushes for the safety of his own closed room. In Les Petites Vieilles there is from the start a feeling of expansion and creative ambition. The narrow streets now wind towards strange delights:

> Dans les plis sinueux des vieilles capitales,
> Où tout, même l'horreur, tourne aux enchantements . . .

Everything is rapid movement; the poet joyously tracks down the old women as they trot through the city; they are 'des êtres singuliers, décrépits et charmants', and round them he conjures up associations 'd'un gout bizarre et captivant'.

In the picture of the old men every detail gives sharpness, rigidity, hostility, menace; the sense of something about to pierce or to crush (the poking stick in the mud and the feet shuffling 'comme s'il écrasait des morts sous ses savates'). The centre of the poem is the savage and mysterious threat, with only an undertone of unstated pity for these wretched, tattered and malevolent beings.

In *Les Petites Vieilles*, the lost past, loneliness and sudden dignity of the old women, and the central theme of imaginative sympathy, might more easily lead to the sentimental: it is the deliberate stress on the grotesque and even the comic that holds the balance between detachment and pity. Baudelaire seems to have tried a *tour de force* in the mingling of extreme tones, and there are lines where stylised nobility perhaps overreaches itself. The passages which convey the most real compassion are precisely those which describe most cruelly. Decrepitude is brought out in the strongest terms: these are monsters, 'brisés, bossus, tordus', shrivelled shadows creeping and tottering, jerky puppets, wounded beasts, helpless bells tossed on a rope. But among all that makes them most mechanical, most animal or most geometrical (see p. 28) they keep the most human feature of all: their eyes, with a piercing outward gaze and the softness of infinite depths:

> ils ont des yeux perçants comme une vrille,
> Luisants comme ces trous où l'eau dort dans la nuit;
> Ils ont les yeux divins de la petite fille
> Qui s'étonne et qui rit à tout ce qui reluit.

Besides evoking the people of the city and mirroring his own feelings, Baudelaire leaves a general suggestion to echo in the reader's mind. The seven mysterious old men (perhaps emblems of the seven deadly sins) call up 'le mystère et l'absurdité' and the old women 'la griffe effroyable de Dieu'. Other poems combine in the same way the picture of something from Paris life, Baudelaire's personal struggle, and the wider sense of human fate. *Les Aveugles* watches the blind fumbling their way along with blank eyes turned always upwards, pauses with 'Vois, je me traîne aussi' and ends with the despairing question: 'Que cherchent-ils au Ciel, tous ces aveugles?' The avid and ageing gamblers cause a piercing envy, envy for those who are totally and actively absorbed even in self-destruction instead of sunk in blank nothingness. In *Danse macabre* the statue of a woman's skeleton dressed for the ball appeals to his love of irony, of the sheer beauty of complex mathematical shape, and of imagining a past, then calls up the old symbol of the dance of death, with corrupt and frivolous mankind capering madly in 'Le branle universel de la danse macabre'.

There are one or two more directly personal poems, on memories of childhood, the search for forgetfulness in physical pleasure, or a sudden moment of fascination in *A une Passante* with its simple and musical last line:

O toi que j'eusse aimée, ô toi qui le savais!

But even in *Le Crépuscule du Soir* and *Le Crépuscule du Matin* which extend over a whole city the complicity and cruelty of evening and morning twilight, Baudelaire suggests the centre of his personal struggles. Among the images for destruction by poverty, crime, debauchery or death comes constantly the theme of stubborn toil. Evening brings relief to thinker, writer and Paris labourer. And in the shivering discomfort of dawn, heavily, laboriously, work sets out once more:

Et le sombre Paris, en se frottant les yeux,
Empoignait ses outils, vieillard laborieux.

8. *Le Vin*

'Il faut être toujours ivre . . . De vin, de poésie ou de vertu, à votre guise', wrote Baudelaire in the *Petits poèmes en Prose* (286). Wine is one of many possible symbols for the desire to transform life.

The section is placed here because the stimulant brings out in heightened form the forces that already struggle in man: his appetite for intense enjoyment, his desire alternately to intensify and to lose his individual consciousness, and his revolt against the imperfection of things as they are. In fostering rebellious pride and giving a sense of godlike ecstasy it leads on to the intensified despairs and desires that will follow.

Wine is a symbol for the complex urges struggling in man; but at the same time, the individual drinkers come alive physically and mentally, from the family of the poor workman invigorated after the week's labour, through the drunken rag-and-bone merchant who staggers home imagining himself a prince or a warrior, to the alcoholic murderer with his confused and cruel love for the wife he has killed.

There are few poems in this section, but they are arranged to open with the pleasures of wine, move through suffering, cruelty and revolt, and return to a dream of delight.

In the first poem, wine consoles, strengthens and gives poetry to life. *Le Vin des Chiffonniers* has a dry comedy in the picture of the rag-pickers bent and battered, yet transported by bellicose visions, made by wine as clumsy as the poet in real life, and like him creating proud and

wonderful dreams. In the first version of this poem Baudelaire had seen
wine as a gift of God; in the poem as it now stands, it has become man's
creation in protest against the world: with its aid he 's'enivre des splen-
deurs de sa propre vertu'. In *Le Vin de l'Assassin* thirst for enjoyment,
desire for oblivion, the will to destroy what one loves and a reckless
defiance reach their paroxysm. Finally, wine intensifies in the poet

> l'orgueil, ce trésor de toute gueuserie,
> Qui nous rend triomphants et semblables aux Dieux,

and in the lover the dream of setting out 'vers le paradis de mes rêves'.

9. *Fleurs du Mal*

The dream of paradise is followed by the thrust back into terror and
disgust: 'Sans cesse à mes côtés s'agite le Démon'. It is in this section that
man's longings for infinite delight or total oblivion reach their utmost
aberrations. In one of his prose poems, at the end of a study of sadism,
Baudelaire was to ask:

> peut-il exister des monstres aux yeux de Celui-là seul qui sait pourquoi
> ils existent, comment ils se sont faits et comment ils auraient pu ne pas
> se faire? (303)

And at the root of man's strangest sins, he says elsewhere, lies 'cette
dépravation du sens de l'infini' (349).

A certain disquiet at the thought of contemporary moralisers seems to
have made many of these poems uneven and led Baudelaire into moments
of defiantly cloying artifice in *Lesbos* or of rhetorical condemnation in
Femmes Damnées — Delphine et Hippolyte (now in *Les Epaves*), but there
are many lines which subtly evoke delight and tenderness:

> Mes baisers sont légers comme ces éphémères
> Qui caressent le soir les grands lacs transparents . . .

then set them by the side of their opposites without the need for explicit
moral comment:

> L'âpre stérilité de votre jouissance
> Altère votre soif et roidit votre peau,
> Et le vent furibond de la concupiscence
> Fait claquer votre chair ainsi qu'un vieux drapeau . . .

The desperate desire for infinite pleasure leads into the search for
oblivion, which would destroy remorse; in *Allégorie* and *Les Deux
Bonnes Sœurs* there is the refrain of 'Un lit que le remords n'a jamais

fréquenté', but in *La Fontaine de Sang* and *Les Métamorphoses du Vampire*
the promise

> je sais la science
> De perdre au fond d'un lit l'antique conscience

is followed by the hideous reawakening.

   The theme of man's substance being eaten away runs strongly through
this section and is at its pitch in *Un Voyage à Cythère*, certainly the finest
poem of this group. Baudelaire here weaves together the suggestions
of joyous adventure, loveliness and grace, the virulently rich sense-
impressions of the decaying corpse pecked and torn by birds and beasts
of prey, and sudden lines of extreme simplicity. The first two stanzas
set sail in radiant light on a soft swell, the feelings soaring like birds
among the rigging of the ship; the delicate dreams of delight are set
moving in 'Cythère . . . un pays fameux dans les chansons . . . Eldorado
. . .' to fall thudding back in 'Eldorado banal de tous les vieux garçons',
followed by the slow and deadly simple:

> Regardez, après tout, c'est une pauvre terre.

The soaring birds become carrion crows and the most piercing words are
used to show rotting corruption devoured and torn to bits. Self-disgust is
conveyed intensely through physical nausea; then the final words move
back to direct simplicity:

> Ah! Seigneur! donnez-moi la force et le courage
> De contempler mon cœur et mon corps sans dégoût!

Even in this despair and decay there is an ineradicable will to face with
strength the knowledge of the nature of things.

10. *La Révolte*

The two themes of wretchedness and of pride, of aspiration and
despair have throughout the book been leading to the climax of revolt
against 'un monde où l'action n'est pas la sœur du rêve'. These poems
are intended to shock, but there is more in them than childish sacrilege.
As so often in Baudelaire, the names of God, Christ and Satan must be
understood less with their orthodox religious meaning than as symbols
for forces that weigh upon or struggle in man.

Le Reniement de Saint Pierre does not consider Christ's death with the
meaning given to it by the Church—redemption in another world—but
makes it the symbol of the desire to transform the present world, tragic-
ally frustrated. This is an early poem, strongly romantic in undertone.

with its picture of a persecuted victim, oppressed by money-grubbers and the mob as well as by a cruel fate. Where it takes on its own originality can be seen if it is compared with Vigny's *Le Mont des Oliviers*; this is not abstract philosophical discussion in epic tone, but is directed to giving the most intimate physical sense of the sufferings endured by Christ and by humanity, and of a gloating, sadistic power behind the universe. In the deliberate simplification of the end there is the bite of successful rhetoric.

In *Abel et Caïn* Baudelaire again takes a theme often treated by the romantics and makes of Abel the comfortable conformist, richly at ease with things as they are, and of Cain the man of vast longings and the rebel against the established order. But of these three poems, none of which is among the very best of Baudelaire, the most suggestive is *Les Litanies de Satan*. This is an incantatory rendering of human desperation and human strivings. Baudelaire has charged his reversed litany with all kinds of traditions of magic running underground throughout the ages. But above all he has made of Satan the image of the two-sided nature of things; for, if he is patron saint to the rebel and consoler to the criminal, it is also he who from imperfection and misery brings hope and the longing for paradise; imperfection is once again the necessary condition for aspiration. The last lines stretch towards the 'Arbre de Science'; the tree of the knowledge of good and evil, forbidden to man; it is to this intensification of knowledge through no matter what experience that the imagination has been striving throughout the *Fleurs du Mal*.

11. *La Mort*

Death forms the conclusion, but not as a simple symbol of failure. Here there are re-expressed in a new context those same conflicting desires and fears that the whole volume has shown. The poems on death follow a typically Baudelairean movement: first the dream of ecstasy with its two sides—enhanced delight or the flooding peace of oblivion; then the terror; and finally the synthesis in *Le Voyage*.

La Mort des Amants evokes the dream of dying together in one flash of ecstasy to be awakened to new delight. *La Mort des Pauvres* moves between the words and music of litany and mysticism and the familiar language and images of everyday life, to show death as both the ecstatic dream and simple peace for the weary. For the artist who struggles endlessly to find perfect expression, death may bring the bursting into flower of all his mind holds.

La Fin de la Journée is in its succinct suggestiveness one of the finest of the *Fleurs du Mal*. Brief and biting, the eight-syllabled lines give the almost gasping effect of a man at the end of his tether; at the same time, one long sentence runs from the fourth to the fourteenth, carrying suspense, expectation and sudden relief. Three lines at the beginning, deliberately split and jerky, convey the garishness and futility of life, a contorted and purposeless dancer under a sickly light, gaudy and importunate. Then after the harsh and the tinselly comes the prolonged, soft, rich movement full of undefined sensuousness as the long adjective trails across the line, and night instead of falling rises in a wave of relief:

> Aussi, sitôt qu'à l'horizon
> La nuit voluptueuse monte . . .

Night blots out the physical need and the mental torture,

> Apaisant tout, même la faim,
> Effaçant tout, même la honte,

and the lines run on into the sudden breath of release with 'Enfin!' Again both mind and body cry out for rest; every separate bone of the spine is stressed and the need becomes a burning prayer:

> Mon esprit, comme mes vertèbres,
> Invoque ardemment le repos . . .

Then at last comes the complete giving in, with the twisting gesture of the body as it wraps itself in safety and comfort, till, in the sudden long adjective stretched across the last line, the shadows bring coolness and peace:

> Je vais me coucher sur le dos
> Et me rouler dans vos rideaux,
> O rafraîchissantes ténèbres!

But the contrast comes in *Le Rêve d'un Curieux*. That death will bring ecstasy or peace is perhaps merely another dream of man. *Le Squelette laboureur* had already suggested the fear that 'tout, même la Mort, nous ment', that 'le sommeil promis n'est pas sûr' and that death may lead to a mere continuance. Baudelaire's tone in *Le Rêve d'un Curieux* is completely his own. Leconte de Lisle had expressed the same terror in a sonnet which is a triumph of ringing rhetoric: 'Après l'apothéose, après les gémonies . . .'; Baudelaire leads to the shock of discovery through the quiet conversational opening: 'Connais-tu, comme moi . . .' and the everyday image of the impatient child in the theatre waiting for the curtain to go up, till there comes the terror of the realisation, the familiar interjection and the blankness of the end:

> J'étais mort sans surprise, et la terrible aurore
> M'enveloppait. —Eh quoi! n'est-ce donc que cela?
> La toile était levée et j'attendais encore.

Le Voyage in its threefold movement looks back over the whole book. Moving out of the serene protected circle of the child poring over maps and prints by lamplight, the imagination sets sail into immensity and can never be satisfied; the travellers return having found only

> Le spectacle ennuyeux de l'immortel péché;

but to the end the appetite for experience and knowledge refuses to be stilled and will set out yet again.

This is Baudelaire's most sustained poem, and every stanza is particularly rich in suggestion. It moves easily through shifts and changes of tone, from the quiet intimate picture of the child to the cosmic vision of the suns in space cruelly whipped like spinning tops, from the conversational irony of

> Pour trouver le repos court toujours comme un fou

and the showman's cry 'Par ici, vous qui voulez manger . . .' to the legendary dignity of 'Notre âme est un trois-mâts cherchant son Icarie', or the deadly and straightforward

> Nous nous sommes souvent ennuyés, comme ici.

All the threads of the book are deliberately recalled and drawn together: the fascination of woman, 'la Circé tyrannique aux dangereux parfums', her frivolity and inability to understand the suffering of others: 'sans rire s'adorant et s'aimant sans dégoût', and yet at the end the setting out to find once again peace with 'celle dont jadis nous baisions les genoux'; the transforming of the outer world by the imagination as clouds shift in lovely shapes or a candle in a hovel seems to light up some scene of luxury; the search for delight or oblivion in drugs; the restlessness, cruelty, pride and self-congratulation of man till he becomes 'ivre de son génie' and rebels against God; his disillusion and his will to continue in one last bitter hope.

The *Fleurs du Mal* have traced the progress of man's creative ambition and the complexities to which it may lead. 'Chacun est le diminutif de tout le monde', said Baudelaire (1222), as Montaigne before him had written 'Chaque homme porte la forme entière de l'humaine condition'. At the roots of all experience he sees the same basic human struggles; between will-power and lethargy, pride and self-loathing, cruelty and tenderness, the creative and the destructive.

In a stanza in *Le Squelette laboureur* he writes of old engravings in books of anatomy:

> Dessins auxquels la gravité
> Et le savoir d'un vieil artiste,
> Bien que le sujet en soit triste,
> Ont communiqué la Beauté.

'La gravité'; the sense of the dignity and worth of human strivings; 'le savoir d'un artiste': the patient skill in expression. It is through these that Baudelaire gives to poetry 'le sentiment de l'existence immensément augmenté'.

Biographical Note

Baudelaire lived from 1821 to 1867. When he was six years old, his father died; and the following year his mother married again, becoming Mme Aupick. Generalisations about his attitude to his stepfather often prove misleading and are irrelevant to appreciation of his poetry. He himself analyses his early life in a letter of 6 May 1861, which is worth consulting. Certainly his family background contributed to two central conflicts expressed in the poems: an intense need for tenderness and comfort, set against scorn of woman as superficial, treacherous and uncomprehending; and a need to shock by his revolt against conventional values, yet a constant sense of personal guilt and shortcoming.

In 1841 General Aupick and his wife, disturbed by the extravagance and dissipation of the young Baudelaire, sent him on a voyage towards India; he reached Mauritius, then returned to France in 1842. The theme of the ship setting sail for tropical seas will provide one of the most suggestive symbols in his poetry. Yet here, as with all his other themes, his poetry does not develop detailed anecdotes from personal experience, but sifts out what can serve to suggest basic human feelings.

His passionate relationship with the mulatto woman Jeanne Duval began on his return; he was to continue to protect her through long years in spite of quarrels, treachery and illness. The facts and chronology regarding his poems and letters to Madame Sabatier and Marie Daubrun, during the 1850's, remain uncertain in detail. In the poems Baudelaire is of course giving not a direct version of his own life-story but the suggestive outline of certain central human experiences. In 1844, disquieted by Baudelaire's debts, Mme Aupick obtained a legal injunction that the management of the money he had inherited should be removed from his control and entrusted to the lawyer Ancelle. For the rest of his life Baudelaire struggled to reach solvency and support himself through his literary works, and constantly failed to do so, in part because of his own disorganisation, in part through the rigour of circumstances. His notebooks, *Fusées* and *Mon Cœur mis à nu*, show his lucid consciousness of the forces at odds within his character: on the one hand procrastination and self-indulgence, exacerbated by the intense difficulty he finds in adequately expressing his experience; on the other the belief in unremitting effort and the conviction that his life will not be wasted if he can produce from it a great work of art.

From 1845 onwards, Baudelaire published remarkable articles of art criticism, a short story *La Fanfarlo*, translations of the works of Edgar Allan

Poe, in whose theories on poetry he finds parallels with many of his own ideas, stimulating studies of many contemporaries, including Gautier, Balzac, Hugo and Wagner, works on drugs as a means of insight into the nature of man (*Les Paradis artificiels*) and some of the prose poems to be collected after his death under the title *Le Spleen de Paris* or *Petits Poèmes en prose*.

The *Fleurs du Mal* were published in 1857; Baudelaire was prosecuted and fined, and six poems had to be withdrawn from the collection. A second edition, with a new order and many additional poems, appeared in 1861. When in the same year Baudelaire thought of standing for election to the French Academy, the scandal was such that he was persuaded to withdraw.

In 1864 Baudelaire left Paris for Brussels, where he hoped to find a publisher, and lectured in Belgium without much success. Swinburne in 1862, Verlaine and Mallarmé in 1865 had published articles recognising his status as a great poet, but as late as 1865 no publisher would risk producing his collected works. From 1861 he had known that his health was seriously undermined by the disease he had contracted years before, which had once already recurred after a supposed cure. In 1866 he was struck by general paralysis and brought back to Paris by friends; he spent the last year of his life unable to move or speak, and died in August 1867.

Suggestions for Further Reading

The collected works have been edited by the following scholars: J. Crépet and Cl. Pichois (Conard, 1922–53, 19 vols.); Cl. Pichois (Club du meilleur livre, 1955–6, and revised Pléiade edition, Gallimard, 1966); Marcel Ruff (Le Seuil, 1968, collection l'Intégrale). The *Correspondance* has been edited by Cl. Pichois (Pléiade, Gallimard, 2 vols., 1973). See also his *Album Baudelaire* (Pléiade, Gallimard, 1974).

For *Les Fleurs du Mal*, see editions by J. Crépet and G. Blin (Corti, 1942—the basic scholarly edition, now being revised by G. Blin and Cl. Pichois, vol I, 1968); A. Adam (Garnier, 1958); H. Lemaitre (Garnier-Flammarion, 1964); J. Pommier and Cl. Pichois, with reproductions of works of art which stimulated Baudelaire's imagination (Club des Libraires de France, reprinted 1966); J. Pommier—facsimile of the 1857 edition with companion volume of commentary (Slatkine reprints, 1968).

For Baudelaire's other works, see the following: *Petits Poèmes en prose*, ed. H. Lemaitre (Garnier, 1958); ed. M. Zimmerman (Manchester University Press, 1968); ed. M. Ruff (Garnier-Flammarion, 1966); ed. R. Kopp (Corti, 1969). *Les Paradis artificiels*, ed. Cl. Pichois (Club du meilleur livre,

1961); ed. M. Ruff (Garnier-Flammarion, 1966). *La Fanfarlo*, ed. Cl. Pichois (Club des Libraires de France, 1959). *Journaux intimes*, ed. J. Crépet and G. Blin (Corti, 1949). For Baudelaire as a critic: editions by Cl. Pichois of *Critique littéraire et musicale* and *Critique artistique* (Bibliothèque de Cluny, 1961 and 1965); H. Lemaitre, of *Curiosités esthétiques; L'Art romantique* (Garnier, 1962); L. J. Austin, of *L'Art romantique* (Garnier-Flammarion, 1966).

Critical works are too many for close discussion here. Suggestions will be found at the end of two useful introductory studies by P. Mansell Jones: *Baudelaire* (Bowes and Bowes, 1952) and H. Peyre: *Connaissance de Baudelaire* (Corti, 1951): these indicate important studies by T. S. Eliot, Paul Valéry, M. Raymond, J. Pommier, R. Vivier. Sartre's *Baudelaire* (Gallimard, 1947) should be balanced by the views of G. Blin in *Baudelaire* (Gallimard, 1939) and *Le Sadisme de Baudelaire* (Corti, 1948). Succinct studies in French include those by Marcel Ruff (Hatier, 1955) and Max Milner (Plon, 1967).

In English, the biography by Enid Starkie (Faber and Faber, 1957) supersedes an earlier work; the books by M. Turnell (Hamish Hamilton, 1953) and D. J. Mossop (Oxford, 1961) are sometimes in different ways controversial; Margaret Gilman's *Baudelaire the critic* (New York, 1943) is excellent. F. W. Leakey's *Baudelaire and Nature* (Manchester University Press, 1969) is a rich chronological study with perceptive comments on many poems. Jonathan Mayne has produced finely annotated and illustrated translations of the art criticism (Phaidon, 1956, 1964, 1965).

New facts and new appreciations are constantly being published. The standard bibliographies (Talvart and Place, Thieme, Dreher and Rolli Drevet) may be supplemented by annual surveys in *The Year's Work in Modern Language Studies* and *Publications of the Modern Language Association of America*, and by the annual bibliographies by R. Rancoeur and by O. Klapp. For the most recent details, see the *Bulletin baudelairien*, published twice yearly since 1965 at Nashville, Tennessee, L. J. Austin: 'Etat présent des études sur Baudelaire' (*Forum for Modern Language Studies*, October 1967), Robert T. Cargo's *Baudelaire Criticism, 1950–1967* (University of Alabama Press, 1968), *Deux Années d'études baudelairiennes, 1966–8* (Supplement to Vol. 39 of *Studi francesi*, Turin, 1969), and *Études baudelairiennes*, ed. R. Kopp and Cl. Pichois (Neuchatel, à la Baconnière, 5 vols. since 1969).

Two general works remain particularly stimulating for understanding and enjoyment of the poetry: J. Prévost's *Baudelaire* (Mercure de France, 1953, reprinted 1966) and L. J. Austin's *L'Univers poétique de Baudelaire* (Mercure de France, 1956).

Index